THE WORLD'S CLASSICS
THEOGONY & WORKS AND DAYS

Hēsiodos (Hesiod) is one of the oldest known Greek poets, possibly the oldest. He lived at Ascra in Boeotia (central Greece) in the late eighth century BC. The earlier of his two surviving poems, the *Theogony*, contains a systematic genealogy of the gods from the beginning of the world and an account of their violent struggles before the present order was established. The *Works and Days*, a compendium of moral and practical instruction for a life of honest husbandry, throws a unique and fascinating light on archaic Greek society, ethics, and superstition. Hesiod's poetry is the oldest source for the myths of Prometheus, Pandora, and the Golden Age. Unlike Homer, Hesiod tells us about himself and his family, and he stands out as the first personality in European literature.

M. L. WEST was born in 1937. He was educated at St Paul's School and Balliol College, Oxford, and is now Professor of Greek at Royal Holloway and Bedford New College, University of London; he is also a Fellow of the British Academy. His many publications include major critical editions of the Hesiodic poems, with commentary (*Theogony*: OUP, 1966; *Works and Days*: OUP, 1978).

W9-BYK-883

THE WORLD'S CLASSICS

HESIOD

Theogony

AND

Works and Days

Translated
with an Introduction and Notes by
M. L. WEST

Oxford   New York

OXFORD UNIVERSITY PRESS

Oxford University Press, Walton Street, Oxford OX2 6DP

Oxford New York Toronto
Delhi Bombay Calcutta Madras Karachi
Kuala Lumpur Singapore Hong Kong Tokyo
Nairobi Dar es Salaam Cape Town
Melbourne Auckland Madrid

and associated companies in
Berlin Ibadan

Oxford is a trade mark of Oxford University Press

British Library Cataloguing in Publication Data

Data available

Library of Congress Cataloging in Publication Data
Hesiod.
Theogony; Works and days.
(World's classics)
Bibliography: p.
1. Hesiod—Translations, English. 2. Gods, Greek—
Poetry. 3. Mythology, Greek—Poetry. I. West, M. L.
(Martin Litchfield), 1937- . II. Hesiod, Works and
days. English, 1988. III. Title. IV. Series.
PA4010.E5T5 1988   881'.01   87-13471
ISBN 0-19-281788-4 (pbk.)

9 10 8

Printed in Great Britain by
BPCC Hazells Ltd
Aylesbury, Bucks.

CONTENTS

Introduction   vii

Note on the Text and Translation   xxiii

Bibliographical Note   xxv

THEOGONY   1

WORKS AND DAYS   35

Explanatory Notes   63

References to the *Theogony* and *Works and Days* are to the lines of the Greek texts edited by M. L. West (OUP, 1966 and 1978). The running headlines in the Translation give the span of lines of the Greek text rendered on the relevant page.

INTRODUCTION

HESIOD is a less familiar name to the general reader than Homer, Aeschylus, or Plato, and no one would claim that he is as great a writer as they. He was nevertheless one of the most famous poets of antiquity, often mentioned in the same breath as Homer as the other main representative of the early world-view. His distinctive qualities were admired by some of the most sophisticated poets of the Alexandrian age (one of the most sophisticated of ages), and in general his influence on Greek and Roman literature, while not comparable with Homer's, was considerable. From the modern point of view he is fascinating for his mythology, some of which can now be traced back to Babylonian origins; for his religious outlook, in which constructive abstract reasoning coexists with traditional doctrine, quaint superstition, and prophetic fervour; and above all for the unique light he throws on the life and society of the archaic Greece in which he lived.

We have no exact dates for him, but we shall not be far wrong if we place his poetic activity in the last third of the eighth century BC. The eighth century was for most of Greece a time of growing prosperity, expanding population, and increasing mobility. Some of the maritime citie. were becoming active in trade and colonization, sending their ships far to the west, to Sicily and up the western coast of Italy, and to the east, to Syria and perhaps occasionally Egypt. Contacts with the civilizations of the orient had been growing slowly since about 900 BC, and after about 770 they grew more rapidly. It is becoming increasingly apparent, with the advance of archaeological discovery and of the study of oriental texts in cuneiform, that Greece received more far-reaching cultural impulses from the east at this period than anyone imagined fifty years ago. One fact that has always been clear and uncontroversial is the Greeks' borrowing of the alphabet from the Phoenicians and their adaptation of it to their own language. So far as can be judged, this took place about or a little before the middle of the eighth century, following many generations of life without writing. Hesiod and Homer still composed in the limpid formulaic style developed by oral poets over the preceding centuries, and we may assume that they still composed primarily with audiences in view, not readers. But the existence of writing now made it possible for poems to be recorded and preserved in a more or less fixed form. Hesiod and Homer were among the first who took advantage of this possibility, and that is why, from our point of view, they stand at the beginning of Greek literature.

The tradition of heroic epic, as represented by the Homeric poems, had been evolving since the high Mycenaean age, well back in the second millennium BC. By the eighth century Ionian poets, perhaps especially in Euboea and other islands of the central Aegean, had brought it to something approaching its final form. One consequence of the increase in communications between different parts of Greece was that this poetry spread everywhere, arousing not only general admiration but also a new interest in the heroic past. We can see the reflection of this in Hesiod, in his passing allusions to heroic legend, especially the legend of the Trojan War and the various legends centred on Argos and Thebes. He may not have known the *Iliad* and *Odyssey* that we know (my own belief is that they were composed later than his poems), but he was certainly familiar with epic poetry about Troy and other subjects. In fact his poems are composed in the same hexameter metre, Ionian dialect, and formulaic diction as those of the Homeric tradition, although he was not an Ionian himself. He must have chosen this style as being the most fitting (or fashionable) for the large-scale poems he wished to compose.

Unlike Homer, he tells us a certain amount about himself and his life. Hence we are able to say that his father came from the Aeolian city of Cyme on the coast of Asia Minor, just south of Lesbos. (Certain occasional traces of Aeolian dialect in Hesiod's work are no doubt to be explained by this.) He had been a merchant seaman, but found it difficult to make ends meet and removed to Ascra, an out-of-the-way village on the eastern side of Mount Helicon in Boeotia, presumably to make a living off the land.[1] Here, it seems, Hesiod was born and brought up, together with his brother Perses.

He became a poet, so he claims,[2] through instruction from the Muses themselves as he tended his lambs, or his father's lambs, on the mountain slopes. The goddesses presented him with a staff as a token of his new role, and told him to sing of the family of immortals. The passage served as a model for a series of later poets who boasted playfully of similar encounters with the Muses or Apollo. It is debatable to what extent Hesiod himself was following a convention, and whether he genuinely experienced a religious vision. It might well be true that it was when he was alone on the mountainside that he realized he had the ability to compose poetry. But he must have listened to many other poets reciting, and they must count as his real instructors.

---

[1] *Works and Days* 633–40.   [2] *Theogony* 22–34.

The *Theogony* fulfils the Muses' initial command. Its subject is the origin and genealogies of the gods, and the events that led to the establishment of Zeus as their king. Hesiod had no doubt heard other poems of similar scope, but he probably added to whatever he took over from his predecessors. For example, it looks as if he has invented the list of names which he gives to the nine Muses (77–9), because the names all seem to be suggested by things that he has been saying about the Muses in the preceding passage. The long lists of Nereid and Oceanid nymphs (243–62, 349–61) may also owe much to his invention.

Altogether his catalogue of gods contains some three hundred names. They fall into diverse categories. Some are gods who were actually worshipped, who had altars and priests assigned to them, or at least received prayers or ritual acts of observance at appropriate times. But there are many who, so far as we know, had no cult whatever. Some of them have a role to play in myth, like Atlas who holds up the sky; others do not, and are mere names to us. A few of these look like inventions to hold the genealogy together, as their names are transparent, like Astraeus the father of the stars. Then there are the components of the physical universe, Heaven, Earth, Sea, the Mountains, the Rivers, the Sun and Moon. All these are treated as gods and put in a genealogical relationship with the rest. Genealogy thus takes the place of cosmogony: Hesiod's only answer to the question how the heaven and earth were created is to say that 'first came the Chasm, and then Earth; and Earth gave birth to Heaven, and the Mountains, and Sea'. Finally, Hesiod's gods include personified abstractions: Death, Sleep, Deceit, Strife, Victory, etc. It comes very naturally to Greek poets to speak about abstractions in personified terms, and sometimes to create graphic little scenes in which they are described moving about and acting in human form.[3] When they are personified they must clearly be classed as gods, not mortals; after all, they are invisible and imperishable, and they have the power to affect human affairs. In their case the genealogical framework can be used to express perceived affinities, as at 226–32:

> Hateful Strife bore painful Toil,
> Neglect, Starvation, and tearful Pain,
> Battles, Combats . . .

Here we see Hesiod systematizing things constructively. In two passages in the later poem, *Works and Days*, we find him creating new goddesses of this category as a result of further reflection. Near the beginning he announces his realization that there is another sort of Strife, a good sort, and he assigns her a place in his system as the elder sister of the bad one. Towards the end (760–4), after warning of the dangerous power of rumour, he remarks that once it gets going it never dies, and this leads him to the thought 'She too is somehow a goddess'.

Interlaced with the genealogies of the *Theogony* are the successive episodes of what has come to be known as the Succession Myth, the tale of the succession of divine rulers. It relates how Heaven was overcome by Kronos, the leader of the Titans, and how the Titans in turn were overcome by the younger gods led by Zeus. It is a story of crude and bizarre acts of violence, of gods castrating, swallowing, and generally clobbering each other in a way that sophisticated readers of Plato's time found strange and unacceptable. We now know that it was not the product of Hesiod's savage fancy, but a Hellenized

---

[3] See, for example, the lines about Right in *Works and Days* 220–4 and 256–62.

version of an oriental myth, other versions of which are represented in a Hittite text of the thirteenth century BC and a Babylonian poem of the eleventh (*Enûma Eliš*, sometimes called the *Epic of Creation*). We cannot say where or how it was first taken over by Greeks, but it seems to have made its way to Hesiod via Crete, where Zeus' birth is placed, and Delphi, where the stone that Kronos swallowed instead of Zeus was exhibited (499).

Another narrative interlude is provided by the story of Prometheus (521–616). This is a myth designed to explain the origins of certain institutions and features of the world as we know it. The practice of eating the meat of the sacrificed animal and dedicating the inedible parts to the gods is explained as the consequence of a trick which Prometheus once played on Zeus. Hesiod's piety will not allow it that Zeus was really deceived, but the story presupposes that he was. Zeus then tried to withhold fire from men so that they could not cook their meat, but Prometheus stole it and delivered it to them: that is how we acquired that unearthly commodity. Finally Zeus decided to contrive a punishment for mankind from which there would be no escape. And so we have women.

The main part of the *Theogony* is prefaced by a hymn to the Muses (1–104); it was the regular practice for a reciter of epic to begin with a hymn to a deity before passing to his main theme. Towards the end of this hymn Hesiod eulogizes kings, and goes on to speak of the power of the poet to make people forget the grief of a recent bereavement. It is possible that this was written for a particular occasion on which it was relevant. In *Works and Days* 650–60 the poet recalls that once he travelled to Chalcis in Euboea for the funeral games in honour of a king Amphidamas, organized by the king's sons, and that he

performed a poem there and won a handsome prize for
it. It is tempting to conjecture that the poem was the
Theogony, or a verson of the *Theogony*. That would
certainly account for the lines in the hymn to the Muses,
and it may be added that the classes of people to whom
he especially recommends the goddess Hecate in 430–42
—kings, warriors including cavalry, competing athletes,
sea-fishermen—must all have been represented in that
audience at Chalcis.

The *Works and Days* is a poem of rather varied content.
Its peculiar title refers to two sections of the text contain-
ing instruction on agricultural tasks and on days of the
month that are favourable or unfavourable for different
purposes; but these two portions together make up less
than half of the whole. An apter title might be 'the
Wisdom of Hesiod'. Overall it can be summed up as a
gallimaufry of advice for living a life of honest industry.

Although clearly intended for a wide audience, the
advice is ostensibly addressed to certain individuals
whose honesty and/or industry leave much to be desired:
to Hesiod's brother Perses, who is said to have taken
more than his share of their father's estate (but also, in
another context, to have been reduced to beggary by his
idleness), and to some 'kings', or local nobles, who are
said to have accepted bribes from Perses and shown him
undue favour in return. In the first third of the poem
Perses and the kings are addressed by turns. Both parties
are exhorted to live righteously, and Perses is also
admonished not to live in idleness but to work for his
bread. To explain why work is man's lot, Hesiod retells in
a modified form the story of Prometheus and the gods'
creation of the first woman. In this version the woman is
identified by name as Pandora, and instead of simply
being mankind's punishment in her own person, as the

ancestress of all mortal women, she here releases all ills into the world by opening a jar in which they had been confined. (Hesiod has in mind the typical Greek storage jar, a clay vessel a metre or more high; it was a confusion by Erasmus that made it into 'Pandora's box'.) This leads on to another famous myth, that of the successive ages or more correctly races of mankind, starting from the golden and ending with the iron. Every reference to a 'golden age' in Western literature and speech derives directly or indirectly from this passage of Hesiod. Immediately afterwards we meet the first animal fable in Western literature—a century before the legendary Aesop is supposed to have lived.

In the remaining two thirds of the poem the kings fade out of sight. Perses is still addressed, but it is now assumed that he accepts the need to work and requires practical instruction on how to set about it. In the 'works' section (381–617) Hesiod goes through the agricultural year from ploughing-time to ploughing-time. His main concern is with cereal culture, but he also takes in vine-growing. The emphasis is on when to begin each task and on being sure to make all the necessary preparations in good time. We are not actually told much about how to do the jobs. Hesiod is writing a poem, not a technical manual: the contrasted descriptive passages about mid-winter and high summer (507–35, 582–96) are purely ornamental, and there are many other memorably picturesque details. The agricultural section is followed by one on seafaring, as the farmer may wish to sell his produce elsewhere. Again the emphasis is on times and seasons. Hesiod has little to teach us otherwise beyond a few simple mottoes. Indeed, he admits to having minimal experience of sailing. Even so he claims to be able to give instruction, 'because the Muses have taught me to make song without limit' (662). This may imply that he is drawing on an existing poetic tradition on the subject, as he no doubt was in the case of agriculture.

The sailing section is succeeded by some rather miscellaneous advice on conduct towards the gods and in various social contexts. It is here above all that we encounter the grandmotherly deposits in Hesiod's mind, taboos and superstitions of everyday life which must have been widely respected at least in certain levels of society but which pass unnoticed in other literary sources. Then comes the almanac of days of the month, which again stands quite alone in early Greek literature. Originally it was followed by a further section on the interpretation of bird omens, but this was condemned as spurious (perhaps unjustifiably) by at least one Alexandrian scholar and has not come down to us.

It must be conceded that the *Works and Days* is a disorderly, often rambling text. It looks as if Hesiod several times extended its scope and added new sections, coming to conceive of the poem as a general compendium of useful advice. Although it appears at first to be composed for one specific situation, the poet's dispute with his brother, a careful study leads to the conclusion that this *mise-en-scène* is a literary device. Perses' circumstances shift between one context and another, according to the needs of the context. The kings disappear once Hesiod has finished with the theme of justice; Perses becomes more and more colourless, and he too disappears after the section on navigation. The fact is that the poem contains advice for people in many different circumstances and cannot be explained from any single personal situation in which Hesiod found himself. Did Perses and the quarrel even exist? We cannot prove it.

But the likelihood is that they did, and that Hesiod took his dispute with his brother and the local rulers as the starting-point for a poem which then took on a life of its own.

Whatever impulse personal circumstances may have given to the composition of the *Works and Days*, it is highly probable that Hesiod knew an established tradition of moral-didactic poetry, and moreover a tradition formed under the influence of oriental culture. For the closest parallels to his poem are to be found in the Sumerian, Babylonian, Hebrew, and Egyptian traditions of wisdom literature whose existence can be traced continuously from about 2500 BC to the early centuries of our era. It is a feature of some of the oriental texts that the instruction they contain comes from a victim of injustice and is combined with reproof and remonstrance; the addressee is someone in need of correction, not merely guidance. Hesiod's poem fits this pattern.

His use of an animal fable also points to oriental antecedents. Although he is the first extant Greek author to show knowledge of such fables, they had had a long history in the Near East, starting with the Sumerians in the third millennium. It was certainly from the Levant that they came to Greece. The Myth of Ages, too, appears to have come from that direction. It seems quite alien to the general Greek idea of the past as reflected in epic and mythological tradition; the inclusion of the race of epic eroes as fourth in the series (156–73) disrupts the scheme of metals and of progressive deterioration, and it is obviously a compromise with Greek tradition. The motifs of successive world ages, shortening of man's life, decline from paradise conditions and from perfect virtue, and metallic symbolism can all be paralleled from oriental texts (Mesopotamian, Jewish, Persian, Indian); some of them are later than Hesiod, it is true, but there can hardly be any question of his having influenced them. Finally, the calendar of good and bad days, unique as it is in early Greece, represents a type of superstition attested in Mesopotamia and Egypt.

All this is very remarkable, and classical scholars have not yet fully adjusted to it. It is surprising—as we were not brought up to expect it—to find so much reflection of oriental literature, mythology, and culture in a Greek poet, and especially in one who lived in an upland village in central Greece, miles from the sea. But as I have said, it was a time when Greece was open to eastern influences of many kinds. Whatever the channels by which they came, it seems that Hesiod was peculiarly well placed to pick them up.

His style and diction are essentially those of all Ionian hexameter poetry, including Homeric epic. He writes more tersely than Homer, but with the same reliance on repeated formulae and on ornamental adjectives and adverbs. Zeus will frequently appear as 'Zeus the resourceful' or 'Zeus who bears the aegis' or 'loud-thundering Zeus', irrespective of context. The earth will be 'the dark earth' or 'the wide-pastured earth' or 'earth the mother of flocks'. All is lucid and straightforward—or almost all. Just occasionally Hesiod will come out with some elevated oracular phrase like 'those who till the surly grey' (sea-fishermen), 'horned and hornless forest-couchers' (animals of the woods), 'do not from the fivebranched . . . cut the sere from the green' (cut your nails). Whether or not this tendency reflects the influence of oracular poetry as composed at Delphi, as some have conjectured, it adds to Hesiod's individual charm. A number of riddling expressions that he uses for animals, like 'the boneless one' for the octopus, 'the knowing one' for the ant, 'carryhouse' for the snail, may belong to the same category, though they could be taken as simply colourful elements of popular language.

In the *Works and Days* Hesiod includes many of what look like pre-existing proverbs and popular sayings. Sometimes they stand out as not entirely apt for the context in which he has put them. In places they come thick and fast, one following another into his mind by association; see, for example, the passage beginning 'Seek no evil gains' at 352.

A feature more characteristic of the *Theogony* is the tendency to give 'etymological' explanations of names. At 195–200, for instance, Hesiod tells us why Aphrodite is called Aphrodite, Cytherea, Cyprus-born, and 'genial', and shortly afterwards he gives us two reasons why Heaven gave his children the collective name of Titans. From the standpoint of a modern philologist some of the explanations are as preposterous as others are self-evident. But we must understand that Hesiod was not trying to do what a modern philologist does. He had no conception of the evolution of language. He was just aware that there is usually meaning in names, and that sometimes they seem mysteriously to express something of the nature or history of the person or thing named. His etymologies are intended to draw attention to these apparently significant relationships between name and object.

One characteristic that unites the two poems is Hesiod's religious attachment to Zeus as the great master of the world and overseer of justice. Zeus overcomes his elders and rivals in the *Theogony* by sheer physical force, but there is no doubt in Hesiod's mind that this was entirely good and right, and that Zeus has organized his universe justly and wisely. In the *Works and Days* Zeus is the subject of the opening hymn which, brief though it is, sets the keynote for what follows:

For easily he makes strong, and easily he oppresses the strong, easily he diminishes the conspicuous one and magnifies the inconspicuous, and easily he makes the crooked straight and withers the proud.

Right is the daughter of Zeus (256), the rule Zeus has laid down for mankind (276–80). He listens to her reports of injustice, rewards the righteous with prosperity, and punishes the unrighteous. Hesiod sometimes feels that injustice is vanquishing justice, yet he has faith in his god: 'I do not expect resourceful Zeus is bringing *this* to pass yet!' (273). The wicked will get their deserts, if not spectacularly in their lifetime, then in the gradual decline of their houses (282–4); or they may bring disaster on their whole community (238–47). Hesiod's tone in such passages has reminded many readers of the Hebrew prophets.

We cannot tell how widely known Hesiod's poems were during his lifetime, but they certainly seem to have been famous within a couple of generations of his death. One consequence of this was that various other genealogical and didactic poems came to be attributed to him, whether by deliberate fraud or simply because he seemed the most appropriate author for anonymous works in these categories. They have mostly perished, except for occasional fragments. One that has survived is the *Shield of Heracles*, a rather inferior narrative poem which can be dated to the sixth century. We also possess extensive fragments of the *Catalogue of Women*, likewise of the sixth century; this was a continuation of the *Theogony*, in five books (three to four thousand lines), dealing with the genealogies of heroes. The women of the title were those with whom gods chose to have intercourse and from whom heroic families consequently descended.

As Hesiod's name attracted genealogical and didactic poems, Homer's attracted heroic epics (at least nine besides the *Iliad* and *Odyssey*). Thus by the fifth century BC, if not earlier, Hesiod and Homer had come to stand, by a sort of shorthand, for the whole body of archaic hexameter poetry. The philosopher-poet Xenophanes of Colophon (*c.* 565–470), wishing to criticize the conventional poetic picture of the gods, wrote 'Homer and Hesiod have attributed to the gods everything that is held discreditable among men—thieving, adultery, deceiving one another'. He seems to imply that Homer and Hesiod, as the oldest known poets, were personally responsible for creating this picture. Later in the fifth century the historian Herodotus (ii. 53. 2) says outright, 'it was these who constructed a divine genealogy for the Greeks and who gave the gods their titles, allocated their powers and privileges to them, and indicated their forms'.

In the early fourth century BC a sophist called Alcidamas composed an entertaining fiction about the poetry competition at Chalcis that Hesiod boasts of having won. Alcidamas made Homer take part in the same event, the contest being between the two of them. At first it seemed that Homer would win. Hesiod set him a series of questions and puzzles, all of which he answered triumphantly. Finally the judge invited each of them to recite the best passage from their poems. Hesiod recited the beginning of his agricultural precepts (*Works and Days* 383–92, 'When the Pleiades born of Atlas . . . all in due season'). Homer recited a splendid description of Greek warriors drawn up in close formation to face the foe (*Iliad*

xiii. 126–33, 339–44). The crowd acclaimed Homer; but the judge awarded the prize to Hesiod, on the ground that the poet who commended husbandry and the works of peace was to be preferred to the one who told of battle and slaughter.

The crowd's preference was that of the ancient world in general, and rightly so. But Alcidamas' championing of Hesiod foreshadows his popularity in the Alexandrian age, when more than one intellectual poet—a little bored, perhaps, with the martial epic he had had drummed into him at school—showed enthusiasm for the didactic poet, or in some cases took him as a mascot. Not that any of them produced anything at all like Hesiod: the didactic poetry of this period consisted of systematic expositions of technical subjects, whether agriculture, beekeeping, astronomy, or some medical topic, without the wide-ranging variety, the moralizing, or the personal framework that characterize the *Works and Days*. But they looked back to Hesiod as the founder of the genre, and emulated his compactness of style. Virgil's *Georgics* really belong in this Alexandrian tradition, and owe more to Alexandrian didactic poets than to Hesiod. Yet it is as the Roman Hesiod that Virgil advertises himself (ii. 176):

> and I sing Ascra's song through Roman towns.

There can be few clearer affirmations of Hesiod's classic status.

NOTE ON THE TEXT AND TRANSLATION

THE Hesiodic poems are preserved in a large number of manuscripts dating from the tenth to the sixteenth century. There are also fragments of about fifty ancient copies from between the first century BC and the sixth AD, but these only cover small portions of the text.

Differences of reading do not generally present serious difficulties. The main textual problem is that of interpolation. Here and there we can identify spurious lines which we know were still absent from many ancient copies. But it is likely that in the *Theogony*, at least, some more substantial additions were made at an early stage (before the fifth century BC) and included in all later manuscripts. Parts of the account of the underworld (726–819) are suspect, and above all the end of the poem. Everything after 942 (the birth of Dionysus) is probably post-Hesiodic, and even before that, from 901 (Zeus' marriage to Themis), there may be a different poet at work, though the subject-matter must correspond to Hesiod's intentions.

The translation is based on the text of my critical editions (*Theogony*: OUP, 1966; *Works and Days*: OUP, 1978). While it is mainly in prose, I have used a verse format for some of the catalogues of names in the *Theogony* (because without rhythm they are nothing), for certain proverb sequences in the *Works and Days*, and for one or two other passages where formal structure is important. If I have sometimes made Hesiod sound a little quaint and stilted, that is not unintentional: he is.

BIBLIOGRAPHICAL NOTE

OF the older translations, the one by A. W. Mair (*Hesiod, The Poems and Fragments*, Oxford, 1908) is still of value for its informative introduction and appendices. It includes the spurious *Shield of Heracles* and such of the fragments of lost poems as were known at that time, and also a rather good sonnet on Hesiod by the translator.

A. R. Burn, *The World of Hesiod* (London, 1936) discusses the poet in his social and historical context. For an excellent and more recent account of the period see O. Murray, *Early Greece* (London, 1980). P. Walcot, *Greek Peasants Ancient and Modern* (Manchester, 1970), draws illuminating comparisons between the values of Hesiod's society and those still prevalent in parts of Greece.

There are good accounts of Hesiod in H. Fränkel, *Early Greek Poetry and Philosophy* (New York and London, 1975), chapter 3; A. Lesky, *History of Greek Literature* (London, 1966), chapter 4; *The Oxford History of the Classical World* (Oxford, 1986), chapter 3 (J. Griffin); *The Cambridge History of Classical Literature*, i: Greek Literature (Cambridge, 1985), chapter 3 (J. P. Barron and P. E. Easterling).

Hesiod's connections with the orient are the subject of a monograph by P. Walcot, *Hesiod and the Near East* (Cardiff, 1966). The introductions to my two editions mentioned above should also be consulted on this topic.

THEOGONY

THEOGONY

FROM the Muses of Helicon* let us begin our singing, that haunt Helicon's great and holy mountain, and dance on their soft feet round the violet-dark spring and the altar of the mighty son of Kronos.* And when they have bathed their gentle skin in Permessos, or the Horse's Fountain, or holy Olmeios,* then on the highest slope of Helicon they make their dances, fair and lovely, stepping lively in time. From there they go forth, veiled in thick mist, and walk by night, uttering beautiful voice, singing of Zeus who bears the aegis,

and the lady Hera of Argos,* who walks in sandals of gold,
and the daughter of Zeus the aegis-bearer, pale-eyed Athene,
and Phoebus Apollo, and Artemis the archer,
and Poseidon earth-charioted, shaker of the earth,
and holy Themis, and Aphrodite of curling lashes,
and Hebe of gold diadem, and fair Dione,
Leto, Iapetos, and crooked-schemer Kronos,*
Dawn, mighty Sun, and shining Moon,
Earth, great Oceanus, and dark Night,

and the rest of the holy family of immortals who are for ever.

And once they taught Hesiod fine singing, as he tended his lambs below holy Helicon. This is what the goddesses said to me first, the Olympian Muses,* daughters of Zeus the aegis-bearer:

'Shepherds that camp in the wild, disgraces, merest bellies:
we know to tell many lies that sound like truth,
but we know to sing reality, when we will.'

So said mighty Zeus' daughters, the sure of utterance, and they gave me a branch of springing bay to pluck for a

staff, a handsome one, and they breathed into me wondrous voice, so that I should celebrate things of the future
and things that were aforetime. And they told me to sing
of the family of blessed ones who are for ever, and first
and last always to sing of themselves.

But what is my business round tree or rock? Come
now, from the Muses let us begin, who with their singing
delight the great mind of Zeus the father in Olympus, as
they tell of what is and what shall be and what was
aforetime, voices in unison. The words flow untiring
from their mouths, and sweet, and the halls of their
father, loud-thundering Zeus, rejoice at the goddesses'
clear voice spread abroad, and the peak of snowy
Olympus rings, and the mansions of the gods. Making
divine utterance, they celebrate first in their song the
august family of gods, from the beginning, those whom
Earth and broad Heaven begot, and the gods that were
born from them, givers of blessings. Second they sing of
Zeus, father of gods and men, how far the highest of the
gods he is, and the greatest in power. And again they
sing of the family of men and of powerful Giants* to
delight the mind of Zeus in Olympus, those Olympian
Muses, daughters of Zeus the aegis-bearer.

They were born in Pieria* to Memory, queen of the
foothills of Eleutherae,* in union with the father, the son
of Kronos; oblivion of ills and respite from cares. Nine
nights Zeus the resourceful lay with her, going up to her
holy bed far away from the immortals. And when the
time came, as the months passed away and the seasons
turned about, and the long tale of days was completed,
she bore nine daughters—all of one mind, their carefree hearts set on song—not far from the topmost peak
of snowy Olympus. There they have their gleaming
dancing-places and their fair mansions; and the Graces*

and Desire dwell beside them, in feasting. Lovely is the sound they produce from their mouths as they sing and celebrate the ordinances and the good ways of all the immortals, making delightful utterance.

So then they went to Olympus, glorying in their beautiful voices, singing divinely. The dark earth rang round them as they sang, and from their dancing feet came a lovely *estampie* as they went to their father. He is king in heaven: his is the thunder and the smoking bolt, since he defeated his father Kronos by strength. He has appointed their ordinances to the immortals, well in each detail, and assigned them their privileges.

This is what the Muses sang, who dwell in Olympus, the nine daughters born of great Zeus,

> Clio and Euterpe and Thaleia and Melpomene,
> Terpsichore and Erato and Polyhymnia and Urania,
> and Calliope, who is chief among them all;*

for she even attends august kings. Whomsoever great Zeus' daughters favour among the kings that Zeus fosters, and turn their eyes upon him at his birth, upon his tongue they shed sweet dew, and out of his mouth the words flow honeyed; and the peoples all look to him as he decides what is to prevail with his straight judgments. His word is sure, and expertly he makes a quick end of even a great dispute. This is why there are prudent kings: when the peoples are wronged in their dealings, they make amends for them with ease, persuading them with gentle words. When he goes among a gathering, they seek his favour with conciliatory reverence, as if he were a god, and he stands out among the crowd.

Such is the Muses' holy gift to men. For while it is from the Muses and far-shooting Apollo that men are singers and citharists* on earth, and from Zeus that they are kings, every man is fortunate whom the Muses love; the voice flows sweet from his lips. Though a man's heart be withered with the grief of a recent bereavement, if then a singer, the servant of the Muses, sings of the famous deeds of men of old, and of the blessed gods who dwell in Olympus, he soon forgets his sorrows and thinks no more of his family troubles, quickly diverted by the goddesses' gifts.

Farewell now, children of Zeus, and grant me delightful singing. Celebrate the holy family of immortals who are for ever, those who were born of Earth and Heaven and of black Night, and those whom the briny Sea fostered; and tell how the gods and the earth were born in the first place, and the rivers, and the boundless sea with its furious swell, and the shining stars and broad firmament above; and how they shared out their estate, and how they divided their privileges, and how they gained all the glens of Olympus in the first place. Tell me this from the beginning, Muses who dwell in Olympus, and say, what thing among them came first.

First came the Chasm;* and then broad-breasted Earth, secure seat for ever of all the immortals who occupy the peak of snowy Olympus; the misty Tartara* in a remote recess of the broad-pathed earth; and Eros,* the most handsome among the immortal gods, dissolver of flesh, who overcomes the reason and purpose in the breasts of all gods and all men.

Out of the Chasm came Erebos* and dark Night, and from Night in turn came Bright Air and Day, whom she bore in shared intimacy with Erebos. Earth bore first of all one equal to herself, starry Heaven, so that he should cover her all about, to be a secure seat for ever for the blessed gods; and she bore the long Mountains, pleasant haunts of the goddesses, the Nymphs who dwell in mountain glens; and she bore also the undraining Sea and its furious swell, not in union of love. But then, bedded with Heaven, she bore deep-swirling Oceanus,*

> Koios and Kreios and Hyperion and Iapetos,
> Thea and Rhea and Themis and Memory,
> Phoebe of gold diadem, and lovely Tethys.

After them the youngest was born, crooked-schemer Kronos, most fearsome of children, who loathed his lusty father.*

> And again she bore the proud-hearted Cyclopes,*
> Thunderer, Lightner, and Whitebolt stern of spirit,

who gave Zeus his thunder and forged his thunderbolt. In other respects they were like the gods, but a single eye lay in the middle of their forehead; they had the surname of Circle-eyes because of this one circular eye that lay on their forehead. And strength and force and resource were upon their works.

And again there were born of Earth and Heaven three more sons, mighty and stern, not to be spoken of, Kottos, Briareos, and Gyges, overbearing children. A hundred arms sprang from their shoulders—unshapen hulks—and fifty heads grew from the shoulders of each of them upon their stalwart bodies. And strength boundless and powerful was upon their mighty form.

For all those that were born of Earth and Heaven were the most fearsome of children, and their own father loathed them from the beginning. As soon as each of them was born, he hid them all away in a cavern of Earth, and would not let them into the light; and he took pleasure in the wicked work, did Heaven, while the huge Earth was tight-pressed inside, and groaned. She thought up a nasty trick. Without delay she created the element of grey adamant,* and made a great reaping-hook, and showed it to her dear children, and spoke to give them courage, sore at heart as she was:

'Children of mine and of an evil father, I wonder whether you would like to do as I say? We could get redress for your father's cruelty. After all, he began it by his ugly behaviour.'

So she spoke; but they were all seized by fear, and none of them uttered a word. But the great crooked-schemer Kronos took courage, and soon replied to his good mother:

'Mother, I would undertake this task and accomplish it—I am not afraid of our unspeakable father. After all, he began it by his ugly behaviour.'

So he spoke, and mighty Earth was delighted. She set him hidden in ambush, put the sharp-toothed sickle into his hand, and explained the whole stratagem to him.

Great Heaven came, bringing on the night, and, desirous of love, he spread himself over Earth, stretched out in every direction. His son reached out from the ambush with his left hand; with his right he took the huge sickle with its long row of sharp teeth and quickly cut off his father's genitals, and flung them behind him to fly where they might. They were not released from his hand to no effect, for all the drops of blood that flew off were received by Earth, and as the years went round she bore the powerful Erinyes* and the great Giants* in gleaming armour with long spears in their hands, and the nymphs whom they call Meliai* on the boundless earth.

As for the genitals, just as he first cut them off with his instrument of adamant and threw them from the land into the surging sea, even so they were carried on the waves for a long time. About them a white foam grew from the immortal flesh, and in it a girl formed. First she approached holy Cythera;* then from there she came to sea-girt Cyprus. And out stepped a modest and beautiful goddess, and the grass began to grow all round beneath her slender feet. Gods and men call her Aphrodite, because she was formed in foam,* and Cytherea, because she approached Cythera, and Cyprus-born, because she was born in wave-washed Cyprus, and 'genial',* because she appeared out of genitals. Eros and fair Desire attended her birth and accompanied her as she went to join the family of gods. And this has been her allotted province from the beginning among men and immortal gods:

> the whisperings of girls; smiles; deceptions;
> sweet pleasure, intimacy, and tenderness.

As for those children of great Heaven, their father who begot them railed at them and gave them the surname of Titans, saying that straining *tight* in wickedness they had done a serious thing, and that he had a *title* to revenge for it later.

Night bore hateful Doom and dark Fate and Death, she bore Sleep, she bore the tribe of Dreams. And secondly gloomy Night bore Cavil and painful Misery, bedded with none of the gods; and the Hesperides,* who mind fair golden apples beyond the famed Oceanus, and the trees that bear that fruit; and the Fates she bore, and the mercilessly punishing Furies* who prosecute the trans-gressions of men and gods—never do the goddesses cease from their terrible wrath until they have paid the sinner his due. And baleful Night gave birth to Resent-ment* also, an affliction for mortal men; and after her she bore Deceit and Intimacy, and accursed Old Age, and she bore hard-hearted Strife.

Hateful Strife bore painful Toil,
Neglect, Starvation, and tearful Pain,
Battles, Combats, Bloodshed and Slaughter,
Quarrels, Lies, Pretences, and Arguments,
Disorder, Disaster—neighbours to each other—
and Oath,* who most harms men on earth,
when someone knowingly swears false.

Sea fathered Nereus,* reliable and true, the eldest of his
children. And they call the old man so because he is *ne'er-
failing* and kindly, and does not neglect what is right, but
has a just and kindly mind. Then again he fathered great
Thaumas and noble Phorcys in union with Earth, and
Ceto of the lovely cheeks, and Eurybia,* who had a spirit
of adamant in her breast.

From Nereus were born numerous goddess-children*
in the undraining sea, and from Doris, lovely-haired
daughter of Oceanus the unending river:

Protho, Eucrante, Sao, and Amphitrite,
Eudora, Thetis, Galene, and Glauce,
Cymothoe, swift Speo, and lovely Thalia,
Pasithea, Erato, and rosy Eunice,
delightful Melite, Eulimene and Agaue,
Doto and Proto, Pherosa, Dynamene,
Nesaea and Actaea and Protomedea,
Doris, Panope, and beautiful Galatea,
lovely Hippothoe and rosy-armed Hipponoe,
Cymodoce, who stills with ease the waves
in the misty sea and the gusts of strong-blowing winds
with Cymatolege and fair-ankled Amphitrite;
Cymo and Eïone and fair-diadem Halimede,
smiling Glauconome and Pontoporea,
Leagora and Euagora and Laomedea,
Polynoe, Autonoe, and Lysianassa,
Euarne lovely of build and perfect to behold,

and Psamathe of charming body, and gracious Menippe,
Neso, Eupompe, Themisto, and Pronoe,
and Nemertes,* who has her immortal father's manner.

These were born of the excellent Nereus, fifty daughters
of excellent attainments.

Thaumas married a daughter of deep-flowing
Oceanus, Electra, and she bore swift Iris* and the lovely-
haired Harpies,* Aello and Ocypeta, who race with the
gusts of the winds and with the birds on swift wings, for
they hurl on high.

To Phorcys Ceto bore old women fair of cheek, white-
haired from birth: the immortal gods and men who walk
on earth call them the Old Women,* fair-robed
Pemphredo and saffron-robed Enyo. And she bore the
Gorgons, who live beyond famed Oceanus at the world's
edge hard by Night, where the clear-voiced Hesperides
are: Sthenno, Euryale, and Medusa who suffered a grim
fate. She was mortal, but the other two immortal and
ageless; and with her the god of the Sable Locks* lay in
a soft meadow among the spring flowers. And when
Perseus* cut off her head from her neck, out sprang
great Chrysaor and the horse Pegasus. He was so named
because he was born beside the waters of Oceanus,
while the other was born with a golden sword in his
hands.* Pegasus flew away and left the earth, the
mother of flocks, and came to the immortals; and he lives
in Zeus' palace, bringing thunder and lightning for
Zeus the resourceful. Chrysaor fathered three-headed
Geryoneus* in union with Callirhoe, daughter of famed
Oceanus. The mighty Heracles despoiled him beside the
shambling oxen in sea-girt Erythea* on the day when he
drove off the broad-browed bulls to holy Tiryns,* after he
had crossed Oceanus and killed Orthos* and the herds-

man Eurytion in the misty ranch beyond famed Oceanus.

But Ceto bore another impossible monster—not like mortal men nor the immortal gods—in a hollow cave, the wondrous Echidna stern of heart, who is half a nymph with fair cheeks and curling lashes, and half a monstrous serpent, terrible and huge, glinting and ravening, down in the hidden depths of the numinous earth. There she* has her cave, down below in a hollow cliff, far away from immortal gods and mortal men, where the gods allotted her a home to dwell.

Grim Echidna is confined underground in the land of the Arimi,* immortal nymph and ageless for all time. And they say Typhaon* was united with her in intimacy, terrible lawless brute with curly-lashed nymph; and she conceived, and bore stern-hearted children. First she gave birth to Orthos, a dog for Geryoneus. Secondly she bore an impossible creature, unspeakable, the ravening Cerberus, Hades' dog with a voice of bronze, fifty-headed, shy of no one, and powerful. Thirdly she gave birth to the baleful Hydra of Lerna,* whom the white-armed goddess Hera fostered in her insatiable wrath towards the mighty Heracles.* But the son of Zeus, called son of Amphitryon,* Heracles, slew it with merciless bronze, with the help of the warlike Iolaus, and the advice of Athene driver of armies.*

But she* bore Chimaera, who breathed invincible fire, a terrible great creature, swift-footed and strong. She had three heads: one of a fierce lion, one of a she-goat, and one of a powerful serpent. She was killed by noble Bellerophon* with Pegasus. But she,* surrendering to Orthos, bore the baneful Sphinx, death to the people of Cadmus,* and the Nemean Lion, which Hera, Zeus' honoured wife, fostered and settled in the foothills of Nemea,* an affliction for men. There it lived, harassing the local peoples, monarch of Tretos in Nemea and of Apesas;* but mighty Heracles' force overcame it.

The youngest that Ceto bore in shared intimacy with Phorcys was the fearful serpent that guards the golden apples* in a hidden region of the dark earth, at its vasty limits. That is the descendance of Ceto and Phorcys.

Tethys bore to Oceanus the swirling Rivers,*

> the Nile, Alpheus, and deep-swirling Eridanus,
> Strymon, Maeander, and fair-flowing Danube,
> Phasis, Rhesus, and silver-swirling Achelous,
> Nessus, Rhodius, Haliacmon, Heptaporus,
> Granicus and Aesepus and wondrous Simois,
> Peneus, Hermus, and flowing Caïcus,
> great Sangarius, Ladon, Parthenius,
> Euenus and Ardescus and wondrous Scamander.

And she bore the holy family of Nymphs,* who nurture men on earth with the lord Apollo and the Rivers, having this function allotted by Zeus:

> Peitho and Admete, Vianthe and Electra,
> Doris, Prymno, and godlike Urania,
> Hippo, Clymene, Rhodea, and Callirhoe,
> Zeuxo, Clytia, Idyia, and Pasithoe,
> Plexaura and Galaxaura, lovely Dione,
> Melobosis, Thoe, and fair Polydora,
> Cerceïs of lovely form, Pluto of big dark eyes,
> Perseïs, Ianeira, Acaste, and Xanthe,
> lovely Petraea, Menestho, Europa,
> Metis, Eurynome, and saffron-robed Telesto,
> Chryseïs, Asia, and desirable Calypso,
> Eudora, Tyche, Amphirho, Ocyrhoe,
> and Styx, who is chief among them all.

These were the eldest daughters born of Oceanus and Tethys; but there are many others too. For there are three thousand graceful-ankled Oceanids; widely scattered they haunt the earth and the depths of the waters everywhere alike, shining goddess-children. And there are as many again of the Rivers that flow with splashing sound, sons of Oceanus that lady Tethys bore. It is hard for a mortal man to tell the names of them all, but each of those peoples knows them that live near them.

Thea, surrendering in intimacy to Hyperion, gave birth to the mighty Sun and shining Moon, and to Dawn, who makes light for all who dwell on earth and for the immortal gods who live in the wide heaven.

With Kreios Eurybia shared intimacy, noble among goddesses, and bore great Astraeus and Pallas, and Perses,* who shone out amongst them all for his wisdom. To Astraeus Dawn bore the stern-hearted Winds, the clearing Westerly and the rushing Northerly and the Southerly, goddess with god bedded in love; and after them the Mist-born one gave birth to the Morning Star, and the shining stars that are heaven's garland.

Styx, daughter of Oceanus, in union with Pallas, bore Aspiration and trim-ankled Victory in her halls, and Power and Strength,* outstanding children, who will not live apart from Zeus, nor take their seats, nor go except where the god goes before them, but they sit for ever beside heavy-booming Zeus. For so did Styx, perennial* Oceanid, determine, on that day when the Olympian Lightner called all the immortal gods to long Olympus, and said that whoever of the gods would fight the Titans with him, he would not smite any of them down from his privileges, but each one would keep the honour he had had before among the immortal gods. And he said that whoever was unhonoured by Kronos and unprivileged, he would set him in the path of honour and privileges, as is right and proper. And the first to come to Olympus was perennial Styx with her children, on the advice of her dear father; and Zeus honoured her, and granted her exceptional favours. He made her to be the great oath of the gods,* and her children to dwell with him for all time. In the same way he fulfilled his promises to all throughout, while he himself has the power and the kingdom.

Phoebe came to Koios' bed of delight; and conceiving then, goddess with god united in intimacy, she bore sable-robed Leto,* ever gentle, mild towards men and immortal gods, gentle from the beginning, most kindly in Olympus. She bore also Asteria,* whom it is good to speak of; whom Perses later brought home to his great house to be known as his dear wife. There she conceived and bore Hecate,* whom Zeus son of Kronos honoured above all others, granting her magnificent privileges: a share both of the earth and of the undraining sea. From the starry heaven too she has a portion of honour, and she is the most honoured by the immortal gods. Even now, when an earthly man sacrificing fine offerings makes ritual propitiation, he invokes Hecate, and great favour readily attends him, if the goddess is well disposed to his prayers, and she grants him prosperity, for she has the power to do so. From all those that were born of Earth and Heaven and were allotted honour, she has a share. The son of Kronos did not oppress her or take away from her anything of what she had been allotted among the Titans, the former gods: she keeps it even as the distribution was first made, from the beginning. Nor does her being an only child mean that the goddess has received less honour and privilege in earth and sky and sea, but much more, because Zeus honours her. By whomsoever she chooses, she comes and stands in full presence and helps him. In time of judgment she sits beside august kings; in the public gathering the man of her choice shines out among the crowd. When men arm themselves for battle and slaughter, there the goddess comes and stands by whichever side she chooses to grant victory with her favour and hand them glory. She is good for standing by cavalry, when she chooses to; and good again when men compete in athletic contest—there the goddess comes and stands by them too and helps them; and victorious by his strength and power, a man wins the fine prize with ease and joy, conferring glory on his parents.* To those too who till the surly grey,* and who pray to Hecate and the strong-thundering Shaker of Earth,* easily the proud goddess grants a large catch; but easily she takes it away when it is sighted, if she so chooses. She is good for increasing the livestock in the folds together with Hermes.* Herds of cattle and broad herds of goats and flocks of fleecy sheep, if so she chooses, she makes great out of small, and less out of many. So, even though she is an only child on her mother's side, she is honoured among the immortals with every privilege. And the son of Kronos made her a fosterer of the young, for those whose eyes since her birth have seen the light of far-sighted day. So she has been a nurse of the young from the beginning, and these are her privileges.

Rhea, surrendering to Kronos, bore resplendent children:

> Hestia,* Demeter,* and gold-sandalled Hera,
> mighty Hades who lives under the earth,
> merciless of heart, and the booming Shaker of Earth,
> and Zeus the resourceful, father of gods and men,
> under whose thunder the broad earth is shaken.

The others great Kronos swallowed, as each of them reached their mother's knees* from her holy womb. His purpose was that none but he of the lordly Celestials should have the royal station among the immortals. For he learned from Earth and starry Heaven that it was fated for him to be defeated by his own child, powerful though he was, through the designs of great Zeus. So he kept no blind man's watch, but observed and swallowed his children. Rhea suffered terrible grief. But when she was about to give birth to Zeus, father of gods and men, then she begged her dear parents, Earth and starry Heaven, to devise a plan so that she could bear her child in secrecy and make Kronos pay her father's furies* and those of the children he had been swallowing, great Kronos the crooked-scheming. And they took heed and did as their dear daughter asked, and told her all that was fated to come to pass concerning Kronos the king and his stern-hearted son. And they told her to go to Lyktos,* to the rich Cretan land, when she was due to bear the youngest of her children, great Zeus. Mighty Earth accepted him from her to rear and nurture in broad Crete. There she came carrying him through the swift, dark night, not stopping until she came to Lyktos, and taking him in her arms she hid him in a cave hard of access, down in the secret places of the numinous earth, in the Aegean mountain* with its dense woods. Then she wrapped a large stone in babycloth and delivered it to the son of Heaven, the great lord, king of the Former Gods.* Seizing it in his hands, he put it away in his belly, the brute, not realizing that thereafter not a stone but his son remained, secure and invincible, who before long was to defeat him by physical strength and drive him from his high station, himself to be king among the immortals.

Rapidly then the lord's courage and resplendent limbs grew; and when the due time came round, the great crooked-schemer Kronos, tricked by the cunning counsel of Earth, defeated by his son's strength and stratagem, brought his brood back up. The first he spewed out was the stone, the last he swallowed. Zeus fixed it in the wide-pathed earth at holy Pytho,* in the glens of Parnassus, to be a monument thereafter and a thing of wonder for mortal men.

He set his father's brothers* free from their baneful bondage, the sons of Heaven whom their father in his folly had imprisoned; and they returned thanks for his goodness by giving him thunder and lightning and the smoking bolt, which mighty Earth had kept hidden up to then. With these to rely on he is lord of mortals and immortals.

Iapetos married a trim-ankled Oceanid nymph, Clymene, and went up to share one bed with her. She bore him Atlas, a stern-hearted child, and proud Menoitios, and Prometheus, subtle, shifting-scheming, and misguided Epimetheus, who from the start turned out a disaster to men who live by bread, since he was the original one who received the moulded maiden from Zeus for a wife. The lawless Menoitios* was sent down to the darkness by wide-seeing Zeus with a smoking bolt, because of his wickedness and overbearing strength. Atlas, under strong constraint, holds up the broad sky with his head and tireless hands, standing at the ends of the earth, away by the clear-voiced Hesperides, for Zeus the resourceful assigned him this lot. And he bound crafty Prometheus in inescapable fetters, grievous bonds, driving them through the middle of a pillar. And he set a great winged eagle upon him, and it fed on his immortal liver, which grew the same amount each way at night as the great bird ate in the course of the day. It was killed by trim-ankled Alcmene's valiant son, Heracles, who saved the son of Iapetos from that affliction and set him free from his distress. Olympian Zeus who rules on

high was not unwilling, intending that the fame of
Heracles, born at Thebes, should be still greater than
before upon the wide-pastured earth: this is why he did
reverence and honour to his eminent son, and, irate
though he was, ended the anger he had before, which
was because Prometheus pitted his wits against the
mighty son of Kronos. For when gods and mortal men
were coming to a settlement at Mekone,* he had carved
up a big ox and served it in such a way as to mislead Zeus.
For him he laid out meat and entrails rich with fat in the
hide, covering it in the ox's stomach, while for men he
laid out the ox's white bones, which he arranged carefully for a cunning trick by covering them in glistening
fat. Then the father of gods and men said to him,

> 'Son of Iapetos, outstanding among all the lords,
> my good sir, how unfairly you have divided the portions.'

So chided Zeus, whose designs do not fail. But crooked-
schemer Prometheus, smiling quietly and intent on
deceit, said to him,

> 'Zeus greatest and most glorious of the eternal fathers,
> choose then whichever of them the spirit in your
>   breast bids you.'

He spoke meaning trickery, but Zeus, whose designs
do not fail, recognized the trick and did not mistake it,
and he boded evil in his heart for mortal men, which was
to come to pass. With both hands he took up the white
fat; and he grew angry about the lungs, and wrath
reached him to the spirit, when he saw the white ox-
bones set for a cunning trick. Ever since that, the peoples
on earth have burned white bones for the immortals on
aromatic altars. In great ire Zeus the cloud-gatherer said
to him,

'Son of Iapetos, clever above all others,
my good sir: then you are still intent on deceit.'

So spoke Zeus in his wrath, whose designs do not fail.
And after that, with his anger ever in mind, he would not
give to the ash-trees the power of untiring fire for mortal
men who live on earth.* But the noble son of Iapetos
outwitted him by stealing the far-beaconing flare of
untiring fire in the tube of a fennel.* And it stung high-
thundering Zeus deep to the spirit, and angered him in
his heart, when he saw the far-beaconing flare of fire
among mankind.

At once he made an affliction for mankind to set
against the fire. The renowned Ambidexter* moulded
from earth the likeness of a modest maiden, by Kronos'
son's design. The pale-eyed goddess Athene dressed
and adorned her in a gleaming white garment; down
over her head she drew an embroidered veil, a wonder to
behold; and about her head she placed a golden diadem,
which the renowned Ambidexter made with his own
hands to please Zeus the father. On it were many designs
fashioned, a wonder to behold, all the formidable
creatures that the land and sea foster: many of them
he put in, charm breathing over them all, wonderful
designs, like living creatures with a voice of their own.

When he had made the pretty bane to set against a
blessing, he led her out where the other gods and men
were, resplendent in the finery of the pale-eyed one
whose father is stern. Both immortal gods and mortal
men were seized with wonder then they saw that precipitous trap, more than mankind can manage. For from
her is descended the female sex, a great affliction to
mortals as they dwell with their husbands—no fit
partners for accursed Poverty, but only for Plenty. As the

bees in their sheltered nests feed the drones, those conspirators in badness, and while they busy themselves all day and every day till sundown making the white honeycomb, the drones stay inside in the sheltered cells and pile the toil of others into their own bellies, even so as a bane for mortal men has high-thundering Zeus created women, conspirators in causing difficulty.

And he gave a second bane to set against a blessing for the man who, to avoid marriage and the trouble women cause, chooses not to wed, and arrives at grim old age lacking anyone to look after him. He is not short of livelihood while he lives, but when he dies, distant relatives share out his living. Then again, the man who does partake of marriage, and gets a good wife who is sound and sensible, spends his life with bad competing constantly against good; while the man who gets the awful kind lives with unrelenting pain in heart and spirit, and it is an ill without a cure.

Thus there is no way of deceiving or evading the mind of Zeus, since not even Iapetos' son, sly Prometheus, escaped the weight of his wrath, and for all his cleverness a strong fetter holds him in check.

When their father* first became hostile towards Obriareos, Kottos, and Gyges, he bound them in powerful fetters, indignant at their overbearing strength and aspect and stature, and settled them below the wide-pathed earth. There they sat at the world's end, living in misery below the earth, at the great world's limits, and for a long time they were suffering there with great pain at heart. But the son of Kronos, and the other immortal gods whom lovely-haired Rhea bore in intimacy with Kronos, brought them up again into the light, on Earth's advice. For she told them everything at length—that with their help they would win victory and their proud claim.

For long they had fought against each other in fierce combat, and the struggle gave them pain at heart, the Titan gods and those that were born of Kronos: the proud Titans from high Othrys,* and from Olympus the gods, givers of blessings, whom lovely-haired Rhea bore bedded with Kronos. They had been fighting each other continually now for ten full years, and the fight gave them pain at heart; and to neither side came solution or end of the bitter strife, and the outcome of the war was equally balanced. But when Zeus provided those allies with full sustenance, nectar and ambrosia, such as the gods themselves eat, and the proud spirit waxed in all their breasts, then the father of gods and men spoke to them:

'Hearken to me, proud children of Earth and Heaven, and let me say what the spirit in my breast bids me. For long now we have been fighting each other for victory and power, day after day, the Titan gods and we who were born of Kronos. But now you must display your great strength and your terrible hands against the Titans in the fearful slaughter, remembering our faithful friendship, and how much you suffered before our decision brought you back into the light from your dismal bondage down in the misty darkness.'

So he spoke, and the excellent Kottos straightway replied:

'Friend, what you say is not unfamiliar to us. We know that you have exceeding intelligence and exceeding insight, and that you have been the immortals' saviour from chilling peril, and that it is by your providence that we have come back up from the misty darkness and our harsh bondage, lord, son of Kronos, after sufferings we never anticipated. So now in turn, with fixed purpose and willing spirit, we will secure your supremacy in the terrible slaughter by fighting the Titans in fierce combat.'

So he spoke, and the gods, givers of blessings, applauded when they heard his words. Their spirits began to yearn for battle even more than before, and they raised such conflict as none would find fault with, all of them, both females and males, on that day, the Titan gods and those born of Kronos, and those whom Zeus brought to the light from the gloom beneath the earth, fearful and powerful ones with overbearing strength. A hundred arms sprang from the shoulders of each of them, and fifty heads grew from their shoulders above their stalwart limbs. These then engaged the Titans in grim slaughter, with sheer cliffs in their stalwart hands, while the Titans on the other side strengthened their battle lines with a will. Both sides displayed a feat of main force; and the boundless sea roared terribly round about, the earth crashed loudly, and the broad sky quaked and groaned. Long Olympus was shaken to its foundations by the onrush of the immortals; the heavy tremors from their feet reached misty Tartarus, and the shrill din of the indescribable onset and the powerful bombardment. So it was when they discharged their woe-laden missiles at each other. The voices of the two sides reached the starry heaven as they called out, clashing with loud battle-cries.

Now Zeus held in his strength no longer. Straightway his lungs were filled with fury, and he began to display his full might. From heaven and from Olympus together he came, with continuous lightning flashes, and the bolts flew thick and fast from his stalwart hand amid thunder and lightning, trailing supernatural flames. All around, the life-bearing earth rumbled as it burned, and the vast woodlands crackled loudly on every side. The whole land was seething, and the streams of Oceanus, and the

undraining sea. The hot blast enveloped the chthonic
Titans;* the indescribable flames reached the divine sky,
and the sparkling flare of the thunderbolt and the lightning dazzled the strongest eyes. An amazing conflagration prevailed over the Chasm: to see it directly with the
eyes and to hear the sound with the ears, it seemed just
as if Earth and broad Heaven above were coming
together, for even such a mighty din would be arising
with her being crashed down upon and him crashing
down from above. So great a din there was as the gods
clashed in strife; and in addition the winds magnified the
quaking and the dust and the thunder and lightning and
smoking bolt, great Zeus' wizardries, and carried the
noise and shouting of both sides together. The din that
rose from the terrible conflict was immense, and it was a
powerful action that was displayed.

The scales of battle turned. But until then, they
attacked each other, fighting furiously in fierce combat.
In the forefront Kottos, Briareos, and Gyges, who was
never sated with battle, raised bitter conflict. Three hundred rocks from their stalwart hands they discharged in a
volley, darkening the Titans' sky with missiles. And they
dispatched them below the wide-pathed earth, and
bound them in painful bondage, having defeated them
by force for all their pride: as far below the earth as
heaven is from the earth, for so far it is from earth to misty
Tartarus. For nine nights and days a bronze anvil might
fall from heaven, and on the tenth reach the earth; and
for nine nights and days a bronze anvil might fall from
earth, and on the tenth reach Tartarus. Round it a brazen
barrier is driven, and darkness is spread about its neck*
in three layers, while above it grow the roots of the earth
and of the undraining sea.

There the Titan gods are hidden away down in the

misty gloom, by decision of Zeus the cloud-gatherer, in a place of decay, at the end of the vast earth. They have no way out: Poseidon fastened brazen doors thereon, and a wall is driven up to the doors from both sides.

There Kottos, Gyges, and brave Obriareos live, trusty guardians of Zeus who bears the aegis.

And there are the sources and extremities of dark earth and misty Tartarus, of the undraining sea and the starry heaven, all in order, dismal and dank, that even the gods shudder at; a vast chasm, whose floor a man would not reach in a whole year if once he got inside the gates, but stormwind upon terrible stormwind would carry him hither and thither. It is a cause of fear even for the immortal gods, this marvel. And there stands the fearful house of gloomy Night, shrouded in clouds of blackness.

Next to that the son of Iapetos* stands holding the broad heaven firmly upon his head and untiring hands, where Night and Day approach and greet each other as they cross the great threshold of bronze. One goes in, one comes out, and the house never holds them both inside, but always there is one of them outside the house ranging the earth, while the other waits inside the house until the time comes for her to go. One carries far-seeing light for those on earth, but the other, baleful Night, shrouded in clouds of mist, cradles Sleep, the brother of Death.

There the sons of gloomy Night have their dwelling, Sleep and Death, fearsome gods. Never does the shining Sun look upon them with his rays when he goes up into heaven, nor when he climbs down from heaven. The one of them ranges the earth and the broad back of the sea gentle and mild towards men, but the other has a heart of iron and a pitiless spirit of bronze in his breast. That man is his whom he once catches, and he is hateful even to the immortal gods.

There, further on, stands the echoing house of the chthonic god,* and in front of it a fearsome hound* stands guard. He is pitiless, and he has a nasty trick: those who enter, he fawns upon with his tail and both his ears, but he does not let them come out again, but watches, and devours whoever he catches going out of the gates.

And there dwells a goddess who makes the immortals shudder,* awful Styx, eldest daughter of Oceanus that flows back into itself. Apart from the gods she has her famed home, roofed with long rocks, and on every side it is fastened to the sky with silver columns. Rarely does Thaumas' daughter, swift-footed Iris, go errands there over the broad back of the sea. When quarrel and strife arise among the immortals, if one of them that dwells on Olympus speaks false, Zeus sends Iris to bring the gods' great oath from far off in a golden jug, the celebrated cold water that drops from a high, sheer cliff and, far below the wide-pathed earth, flows from the holy river through dark night, a branch of Oceanus. A tenth part is her share: nine parts Oceanus winds round the earth and the broad back of the sea with his silver eddies, and falls into the brine, while that one part issues forth from the cliff, a great bane to the gods. Whosoever of the immortals that possess the peak of snowy Olympus swears false upon making a libation of that water, he lies without breathing for a full year, and never lays hands on ambrosia and nectar by way of food, but lies breathless and voiceless on his bed, wrapped in a malignant coma. When he completes his long year of malady, another more trying ordeal succeeds the first. For nine years he is cut off from the gods who are for ever, and does not join them once in council or feast for nine whole years; but in the tenth he rejoins the company of the immortals who dwell in

Olympus. Such is the oath the gods have made of Styx's perennial water—elemental water, that flows through a rugged region.

There are the sources and extremities of dark earth and misty Tartarus, of the undraining sea and the starry heaven, all in order, dismal and dank, that even the gods shudder at; and there are the shining gates and the bronze threshold, firmly fixed with long roots, made by no craftsman's hand. And beyond, excluded from the company of gods, the Titans live, on the far side of the gloomy Chasm. But the renowned allies of loud-crashing Zeus have their home at Oceanus' foundations—Kottos and Gyges; but Briareos was so worthy that the heavy-booming Shaker of Earth made him his son-in-law, giving him his daughter Cymopolea* in marriage.

Now when Zeus had driven the Titans out of heaven, the huge Earth bore as her youngest child Typhoeus, being united in intimacy with Tartarus by golden Aphrodite. His arms are employed in feats of strength, and the legs of the powerful god are tireless. Out of his shoulders came a hundred fearsome snake-heads with black tongues flickering, and the eyes in his strange heads flashed fire under the brows; and there were voices in all his fearsome heads, giving out every kind of indescribable sound. Sometimes they uttered as if for the gods' understanding, sometimes again the sound of a bellowing bull whose might is uncontainable and whose voice is proud, sometimes again of a lion who knows no restraint, sometimes again of a pack of hounds, astonishing to hear; sometimes again he hissed; and the long mountains echoed beneath. A thing past help would have come to pass that day, and he would have become king of mortals and immortals, had the father of gods and men not taken sharp notice. He thundered hard and stern, and the earth rang fearsomely round about, and the broad heaven above, the sea and Oceanus' stream and the realms of chaos. Great Olympus quaked under the immortal feet of the lord as he went forth, and the earth groaned beneath him. A conflagration held the violet-dark sea in its grip, both from the thunder and lightning and from the fire of the monster, from the tornado winds and the flaming bolt. All the land was seething, and sky, and sea; long waves raged to and fro about the headlands from the onrush of the immortals, and an uncontrollable quaking arose. Hades was trembling, lord of the dead below, and so were the Titans down in Tartarus with Kronos in their midst, at the incessant clamour and the fearful fighting.

When Zeus had accumulated his strength, then, and taken his weapons, the thunder, lightning, and smoking bolt, he leapt from Olympus and struck, and he scorched all the strange heads of the dreadful monster on every side. When he had overcome him by belabouring him with his blows, Typhoeus collapsed crippled, and the huge earth groaned. Flames shot from the thunderstruck lord where he was smitten down, in the mountain glens of rugged Aïdna.* The huge earth burned far and wide with unbelievable heat, melting like tin that is heated by the skill of craftsmen in crucibles with bellow-holes, or as iron, which is the strongest substance, when it is overpowered by burning fire in mountain glens, melts in the divine ground* by Hephaestus' craft: even so was the earth melting in the glare of the conflagration. And vexed at heart Zeus flung Typhoeus into broad Tartarus.

From Typhoeus are the strong winds that blow wet, except for the Southerly and the Northerly and the clearing Westerly: these are from the gods by birth, a great blessing to mortals, but the other winds blow haphazard on the sea. Falling upon the misty waves, a great bane to mortals, they rage with evil gusts; they blow different at different times, scattering ships and drowning sailors. There is no help against disaster for men who meet with them at sea. And some of them even on land, the boundless realm of flowers, destroy the fair husbandry of earthborn men, filling it with dust and troublesome refuse.

When the blessed gods had completed their work and settled the matter of privileges with the Titans by force, then on Earth's advice they urged that Olympian Zeus the wide-seeing should be king and lord of the immortals. And he allotted them privileges satisfactorily.

Zeus as king of the gods made Metis* his first wife, the wisest among gods and mortal men. But when she was about to give birth to the pale-eyed goddess Athene, he tricked her deceitfully with cunning words and put her away in his belly on the advice of Earth and starry Heaven. They advised him in this way so that no other of the gods, the eternal fathers, should have the royal station instead of Zeus. For from Metis it was destined that clever children should be born: first a pale-eyed daughter, Tritogeneia,* with courage and sound counsel equal to her father's, and then a son she was to bear, king of gods and men,* one proud of heart. But Zeus put her away in his belly first, so that the goddess could advise him of what was good or bad.

Second he married sleek Themis,* who bore the Watchers,* Lawfulness, Justice, and flourishing Peace, who watch over the works of mortal men; and the Fates, to whom Zeus the resourceful gave the most privilege, Clotho, Lachesis, and Atropos, who give mortal men both good and ill.

Eurynome, a daughter of Oceanus with lovely looks, bore him the three Graces, Aglaïa, Euphrosyne, and fair Thalia.* From their eyes love that dissolves the flesh seeped down as they looked; beautiful is their glance from under their brows.

And he came to the bed of Demeter abundant in nourishment, and she bore the white-armed Persephone, whom Aïdoneus* stole from her mother, Zeus the resourceful granting her to him.

Again, he took love of Memory with her beautiful hair, from whom the Muses with their gold diadems were born to him, nine of them, whose pleasure is in feasts and the delights of song.

Leto gave birth to Apollo and Artemis the archer —lovely children above all the Celestials—in shared intimacy with Zeus who bears the aegis.

Last of all he made Hera his fertile wife, and she bore Hebe and Ares and Eileithyia,* sharing intimacy with the king of gods and men.

And by himself, out of his head, he fathered the pale-eyed Tritogeneia, the fearsome rouser of the fray, leader of armies, the lady Atrytone,* whose pleasure is in war and the clamour of battle; while Hera, furying and quarrelling with her husband, gave birth to the renowned Hephaestus, who is endowed with skills beyond all the Celestials.

From Amphitrite and the loud-booming Shaker of Earth great Triton was born, whose strength extends widely, who occupies the bottom of the sea, dwelling in a golden house with his dear mother and the lord his father; a formidable god.

To Ares the piercer of shield-hides Cytherea bore Terror and Fear, formidable gods who rout tight battle-lines in the chilling conflict together with Ares sacker of cities; and Harmonia, whom proud Cadmus made his wife.*

To Zeus Atlas' daughter Maia* bore glorious Hermes, the herald of the immortals, after going up to his holy bed.

Cadmus' daughter Semele bore him a resplendent son in shared intimacy, merry Dionysus,* immortal son of mortal morther, but now they are both gods.

Alcmene bore the mighty Heracles, in shared intimacy with Zeus the cloud-gatherer.

Hephaestus, the renowned Ambidexter, made Aglaïa his fertile wife, the youngest of the Graces.

Golden-haired Dionysus made auburn Ariadne, Minos' daughter,* his fertile wife, and the son of Kronos made her immortal and ageless for him.

Fair-ankled Alcmene's valiant son, the mighty Heracles, after completing his oppressive ordeals,* made Hebe his modest wife in snowy Olympus, child of great Zeus and gold-sandalled Hera; fortunate Heracles, who performed a great feat among the immortals,* and now lives free from trouble, free from old age, for all time.*

To the tireless Sun the renowned Oceanid Perseïs bore Circe* and king Aeetes.* Aeetes, son of the Sun who makes light for mortals, married by the gods' design another daughter of Oceanus the unending river, fair-cheeked Idyia; and she bore him the trim-ankled Medea, surrendering in intimacy through golden Aphrodite.

Farewell now, you dwellers in Olympus, and you islands, continents, and the salt sea between. But now, Olympian Muses, sweet of utterance, daughters of aegis-bearing Zeus, sing of the company of goddesses, all those who were bedded with mortal men, immortal themselves, and bore children resembling the gods.

Demeter, noble among goddesses, gave birth to Wealth,* in union of intimate desire with the hero Iasius in a thrice-turned fallow field, in the rich Cretan land: Wealth, a goodly god, who goes over all the earth and the broad back of the sea, and whoever encounters him, into whosever hands he comes, he makes him rich and bestows much fortune upon him.

To Cadmus Harmonia, daughter of golden Aphrodite, bore Ino, Semele, and fair-cheeked Agaue,* and Autonoe whom Aristaeus* of the luxuriant hair married, and Polydorus,* in well-walled Thebes.

Oceanus' daughter Callirhoe, sharing golden Aphrodite's intimacy with stout-hearted Chrysaor, bore a son, the strongest of all mortals, Geryoneus, whom mighty Heracles killed for his shambling oxen in sea-girt Erythea.*

To Tithonus* Dawn bore Memnon, bronze-armoured king of the Ethiopians,* and the lord Emathion.* And to Cephalus* she produced a resplendent son, doughty Phaëthon,* a man resembling the gods. While he was young and still had the delicate bloom of his glorious prime, a boy with childish thoughts, Aphrodite the lover of smiles snatched him away and made him her closet servant in her holy temple, a noble Hero.

The son of Aeson* took from Aeetes the daughter* of that Zeus-fostered king by the design of the gods, the eternal fathers, after completing the many oppressive ordeals enjoined upon him by the great overbearing king, the brute Pelias,* who was wicked and stern in action. Having completed them, Aeson's son reached Iolcus after long sufferings, bringing the curly-lashed girl on his swift ship, and made her his fertile wife. And surrendering to Jason shepherd of peoples, she bore a son, Medeios,* whom Chiron the son of Philyra* brought up in the mountains in fulfilment of great Zeus' purpose.

As for the daughters of Nereus, the Old Man of the Sea, Psamathe, noble among goddesses, bore Phocus* in shared intimacy with Aeacus* through golden Aphrodite, while the silverfoot goddess Thetis, surrendering to Peleus, gave birth to Achilles lionheart, breaker of men.

Cytherea with the fair diadem bore Aeneas in union of intimate desire with the hero Anchises* among the peaks and glens of windy Ida.

Circe, daughter of the Sun, the son of Hyperion, in shared intimacy with Odysseus* the enduring of heart, bore Agrius and Latinus, the excellent and strong, who were lords of all the famous Tyrrhenians far away in a remote part of the Holy Isles.* And Calypso,* noble among goddesses, bore Nausithous and Nausinous to Odysseus in union of intimate desire.

These were bedded with mortal men, immortal themselves, and bore children resembling the gods.

WORKS AND DAYS

WORKS AND DAYS

MUSES from Pieria, who glorify by songs, come to me, tell of Zeus your father in your singing. Because of him mortal men are unmentioned and mentioned, spoken and unspoken of, according to great Zeus' will. For easily he makes strong, and easily he oppresses the strong, easily he diminishes the conspicuous one and magnifies the inconspicuous, and easily he makes the crooked straight and withers the proud—Zeus who thunders on high, who dwells in the highest mansions. O hearken as thou seest and hearest, and make judgment straight with righteousness, Lord; while I should like to tell Perses words of truth.

I see there is not only one Strife-brood on earth,* there are two. One would be commended when perceived, the other is reprehensible, and their tempers are distinct. The one promotes ugly fighting and conflict, the brute: no mortal is fond of her, but they are forced by the gods' designs to do homage to Strife the burdensome. But the other was elder born of gloomy Night, and the son of Kronos, the high-seated one who dwells in heaven, set her in the earth's roots, much the better for men. She rouses even the shiftless one to work. For when someone whose work falls short looks towards another, towards a rich man who hastens to plough and plant and manage his household well, then neighbour vies with neighbour as he hastens to wealth: this Strife is good for mortals.

So potter is piqued with potter, joiner with joiner,
beggar begrudges beggar, and singer singer.

Perses, lay this down in your heart, and may the Strife who exults in misfortune not keep your heart from work, a spectator of disputes, a listener at the debate. Little business has a man with disputes and debates who has not food for the year laid up at home in its ripeness, produce of the earth, Demeter's grain. When you have got an abundance of that you can promote disputes and conflict over other men's property. But you will not be able to behave so another time. Instead, without more trouble, let us settle our dispute with straight judgments, the best that Zeus sends. For we divided our estate before, and you kept grabbing and taking much more, paying great tribute to the lords, those bribe-swallowers, who see fit to make this their judgment. The infants, they do not know how much more the half is than the whole, nor how much good there is in mallow and asphodel.* For the gods keep men's food concealed: otherwise you would easily work even in a day enough to provide you for the whole year without working. Soon you would stow your rudder up in the smoke,* and the business of oxen and toiling mules would disappear.

But Zeus concealed it, angry because Prometheus' crooked cunning had tricked him.* On that account he devised grim cares for mankind; he concealed fire. The noble son of Iapetos stole it back for men from Zeus the resourceful in the tube of a fennel, eluding the eye of Zeus whose sport is thunder. In anger Zeus the cloud-gatherer spoke to him:

'Son of Iapetos, clever above all others, you are pleased at having stolen fire and outwitted me—a great calamity both for yourself and for men to come. To set against the fire I shall give them an affliction in which they will all delight as they embrace their own misfortune.'

So saying, the father of gods and men laughed aloud; and he told renowned Hephaestus at once to mix earth with water, to add in a human voice and strength, and to

model upon the immortal goddesses' aspect the fair
lovely form of a maiden. Athene he told to teach her
crafts, to weave the embroidered web, and golden
Aphrodite to shower charm about her head, and painful
yearning and consuming obsession;* to put in a bitch's
mind and a knavish nature, that was his instruction to
Hermes the go-between, the dog-killer.*

So he ordered, and they all obeyed the lord Zeus son of
Kronos. At once the renowned Ambidexter moulded
from earth the likeness of a modest maiden by Kronos'
son's design, and the pale-eyed goddess Athene dressed
and adorned her. The Graces and the lady Temptation
put necklaces of gold about her body, and the lovely-
haired spirits of ripeness garlanded her about with
spring flowers. Pallas Athene arranged all the adorn-
ment on her body. In her breast the Go-between, the
dog-killer, fashioned lies and wily pretences and a
knavish nature by deep-thundering Zeus' design; and he
put in a voice, did the herald of the gods, and he named
this woman Pandora, Allgift, because all the dwellers on
Olympus made her their gift—a calamity for men who
live by bread.

When he had completed the precipitous, unmanage-
able trap, the father sent the renowned dog-killer to
Epimetheus taking the gift, swift messenger of the gods.
Epimetheus gave no thought to what Prometheus had
told him, never to accept a gift from Olympian Zeus but
to send it back lest some affliction befall mortals: he
accepted, and had the bane before he realized it.

For formerly the tribes of men on earth lived remote
from ills, without harsh toil and the grievous sicknesses
that are deadly to men. But the woman unstopped the jar
and let it all out, and brought grim cares upon mankind.
Only Hope remained there* inside in her secure dwelling,

under the lip of the jar, and did not fly out, because the woman put the lid back in time by the providence of Zeus the cloud-gatherer who bears the aegis. But for the rest, countless troubles roam among men: full of ills is the earth, and full the sea. Sicknesses visit men by day, and others by night, uninvited, bringing ill to mortals, silently, because Zeus the resourceful deprived them of voice. Thus there is no way to evade the purpose of Zeus.

If you like, I will summarize another tale for you, well and skilfully—mind you take it in—telling how gods and mortal men have come from the same starting-point.

The race of men that the immortals who dwell on Olympus made first of all was of gold. They were in the time of Kronos, when he was king in heaven; and they lived like gods, with carefree heart, remote from toil and misery. Wretched old age did not affect them either, but with hands and feet ever unchanged they enjoyed themselves in feasting, beyond all ills, and they died as if overcome by sleep. All good things were theirs, and the grain-giving soil bore its fruits of its own accord in unstinted plenty, while they at their leisure harvested their fields in contentment amid abundance. Since the earth covered up that race, they have been divine spirits by great Zeus' design, good spirits on the face of the earth, watchers over mortal men, bestowers of wealth: such is the kingly honour that they received.

A second race after that, much inferior, the dwellers on Olympus made of silver. It resembled the golden one neither in body nor in disposition. For a hundred years a boy would stay in the care of his mother, playing childishly at home; but after reaching adolescence and the appointed span of youthful manhood, they lived but a little time, and in suffering, because of their witless-.ess. For they could not restrain themselves from crimes against each other, and they would not serve the immortals or sacrifice on the sacred altars of the blessed ones, as is laid down for men in their various homelands. They were put away by Zeus son of Kronos, angry because they did not offer honour to the blessed gods who occupy Olympus. Since the earth covered up this race in its turn, they have been called the mortal blessed below, second in rank, but still they too have honour.*

Then Zeus the father made yet a third race of men, of bronze, not like the silver in anything. Out of ash-trees he made them, a terrible and fierce race, occupied with the woeful works of Ares and with acts of violence, no eaters of corn,* their stern hearts being of adamant; unshapen hulks, with great strength and indescribable arms growing from their shoulders above their stalwart bodies. They had bronze armour, bronze houses, and with bronze they laboured, as dark iron was not available.* They were laid low by their own hands, and they went to chill Hades' house of decay leaving no names: mighty though they were, dark death got them, and they left the bright sunlight.

After the earth covered up this race too, Zeus son of Kronos made yet a fourth one upon the rich-pastured earth, a more righteous and noble one, the godly race of the heroes who are called demigods,* our predecessors on the boundless earth. And as for them, ugly war and fearful fighting destroyed them, some below seven-gated Thebes, the Cadmean country, as they battled for Oedipus' flocks,* and others it led in ships over the great abyss of the sea to Troy on account of lovely-haired Helen. There some of them were engulfed by the consummation of death, but to some Zeus the father, son of Kronos, granted a life and home apart from men, and settled them at the ends of the earth. These dwell with carefree heart in the Isles of the Blessed Ones, beside deep-swirling Oceanus: fortunate Heroes, for whom the grain-giving soil bears its honey-sweet fruits thrice a year.*

Would that I were not then among the fifth men, but either dead earlier or born later! For now it is a race of iron; and they will never cease from toil and misery by day or night, in constant distress, and the gods will give them harsh troubles. Nevertheless, even they shall have good mixed with ill. Yet Zeus will destroy this race of men also, when at birth they turn out grey at the temples. Nor will father be like children nor children to father, nor guest to host or comrade to comrade, nor will a brother be friendly as in former times. Soon they will cease to respect their ageing parents, and will rail at them with harsh words, the ruffians, in ignorance of the gods' punishment; nor are they likely to repay their ageing parents for their nurture. Fist-law men; one will sack another's town, and there will be no thanks for the man who abides by his oath or for the righteous or worthy man, but instead they will honour the miscreant and the criminal. Law and decency will be in fists. The villain will do his better down by telling crooked tales, and will swear his oath upon it. Men in their misery will everywhere be dogged by the evil commotions of that Envy who exults in misfortune with a face full of hate. Then verily off to Olympus from the wide-pathed earth, veiling their fair faces with white robes, Decency and Moral Disapproval will go to join the family of the immortals, abandoning mankind; those grim woes will remain for mortal men, and there will be no help against evil.

Now I will tell a fable to the lords, although they can think for themselves. Here is how the hawk addressed the dapple-throat nightingale as he carried her high in the clouds, grasping her in his claws; impaled on the curved talons, she was weeping piteously, but he addressed her sternly:

'Goodness, why are you screaming? You are in the power of one much superior, and you will go whichever way I take you, singer though you are. I will make you my dinner if I like, or let you go. He is a fool who seeks to compete against the stronger: he both loses the struggle and suffers injury on top of insult.'

So spoke the swift-flying hawk, the great winged bird. But you, Perses, must hearken to Right and not promote violence. For violence is bad for a lowly man; not even a man of worth can carry it easily, but he sinks under it when he runs into Blights.* The road on the other side gives better passage, to righteousness: Right gets the upper hand over violence in the end. The fool learns only by experience. For Oath at once runs level with crooked judgments;* there is angry murmuring when Right is dragged off wherever bribe-swallowers choose to take her as they give judgment with crooked verdicts; and she follows weeping to those people's town and territories clad in darkness, bringing ill to men who drive her out and do not dispense her straight.

As for those who give straight judgments to visitors and to their own people and do not deviate from what is just, their community flourishes, and the people blooms in it. Peace is about the land, fostering the young, and wide-seeing Zeus never marks out grievous war as their portion. Neither does Famine attend straight-judging men, nor Blight, and they feast on the crops they tend. For them Earth bears plentiful food, and on the mountains the oak carries acorns at its surface and bees at its centre.* The fleecy sheep are laden down with wool; the womenfolk bear children that resemble their parents;

they enjoy a continual sufficiency of good things. Nor do they ply on ships, but the grain-giving ploughland bears them fruit.

But for those who occupy themselves with violence and wickedness and brutal deeds, Kronos' son, wide-seeing Zeus, marks out retribution. Often a whole community together suffers in consequence of a bad man who does wrong and contrives evil. From heaven Kronos' son brings disaster upon them, famine and with it plague, and the people waste away. The womenfolk do not give birth, and households decline, by Olympian Zeus' design. At other times again he either destroys those men's broad army or city wall, or punishes their ships at sea.

You too, my lords, attend to this justice-doing of yours. For close at hand among men there are immortals taking note of all those who afflict each other with crooked judgments, heedless of the gods' punishment. Thrice countless are they on the rich-pastured earth, Zeus' immortal watchers of mortal men, who watch over judgments and wickedness, clothed in darkness, travelling about the land on every road. And there is that maiden Right, daughter of Zeus, esteemed and respected by the gods in Olympus; and whenever someone does her down with crooked abuse, at once she sits by Zeus her father, Kronos' son, and reports the men's unrighteous mind, so that the people may pay for the crimes of their lords who balefully divert justice from its course by pronouncing it crooked. Beware of this, lords, and keep your pronouncements straight, you bribe-swallowers, and forget your crooked judgments altogether.

A man fashions ill for himself who fashions ill for another, and the ill design is most ill for the designer.

The eye of Zeus, that sees everything and notices everything, observes even this situation if it chooses, and does not fail to perceive what kind of justice even this is that the community has within it. As things are, I cannot wish to be righteous in my dealings with men, either myself or a son of mine, since it is bad to be a righteous man if the less righteous is to have the greater right. Only I do not expect resourceful Zeus is bringing *this* to pass yet!

But you, Perses, must take in what I say and hearken to Right, forgetting force altogether. For this was the rule for men that Kronos' son laid down: whereas fish and beasts and flying birds would eat one another, because Right is not among them, to men he gave Right, which is much the best in practice. For if a man is willing to say what he knows to be just, to him wide-seeing Zeus gives prosperity; but whoever deliberately lies in his sworn testimony, therein, by injuring Right, he is blighted past healing; his family remains more obscure thereafter, while the true-sworn man's line gains in worth.

I will speak to you as a friend, foolish Perses. Inferiority can be got in droves, easily: the road is smooth, and she lives very near. But in front of Superiority the immortal gods set sweat; it is a long and steep path to her, and rough at first. But when one reaches the top, then it is easy, for all the difficulty.

Best of all is the man who perceives everything himself, taking account of what will be better in the long run and in the end. Good is he, too, who follows good advice. But he who neither perceives by himself nor takes in a lesson from another, he on the other hand is a worthless man. But you, ever bearing my instruction in mind, must work, Perses, you who are of Zeus' stock,* so that Hunger may shun you and august fair-crowned Demeter favour you and fill your granary with substance; for

Hunger goes always with a workshy man. Gods and men disapprove of that man who lives without working, like in temper to the blunt-tailed drones who wear away the toil of the bees, eating it in idleness. You should embrace work-tasks in their due order, so that your granaries may be full of substance in its season. It is from work that men are rich in flocks and wealthy, and a working man is much dearer to the immortals. Work is no reproach, but not working is a reproach; and if you work, it will readily come about that a workshy man will envy you as you become wealthy. Wealth brings worth and prestige. But whatever your fortune, work is preferable, that is, if you turn your blight-witted heart from others' possessions towards work and show concern for livelihood as I tell you.

> Inhibition is no good provider for a needy man,
> Inhibition, which does men great harm and great good.
> Inhibition attaches to poverty, boldness to wealth.

Property is not for seizing: far better God-given. For if a man does seize wealth by force of his hands, or appropriates it by means of words—the sort of thing that often happens when profit deludes men's minds, and Shamelessness drives away Shame—the gods easily bring him low, and diminish that man's house, and it is but a short time that prosperity attends him. It is the same if a man does wrong by a suppliant or a visitor; or if he mounts his own brother's bed in secret union with his wife in breach of all propriety; or it in his folly he wrongs someone's orphan children, or if he rails at his old father on the ugly threshold of age, assaulting him with harsh words. With that man Zeus himself is indignant, and in the end he imposes a harsh return for his unrighteous actions.

But you must restrain your blight-witted heart altogether from those things. Make sacrifice to the immortal
gods according to your means in holy purity, and burn
gleaming thighbones; and at other times propitiate them
with libations and oblations, both when you go to bed
and when the divine light returns, so that they may have
a propitious heart and mind towards you, that you may
negotiate for others' allotments, not another man for
yours.

Invite to dinner him who is friendly, and leave your
enemy be; and invite above all him who lives near you.
For if something untoward happens at your place,
neighbours come ungirt, but relations have to gird themselves.* A bad neighbour is as big a bane as a good one is
a boon: he has got good value who has got a good
neighbour. Nor would a cow be lost, but for a bad
neighbour. Get good measure from your neighbour, and
give good measure back, with the measure itself and
better if you can, so that when in need another time you
may find something to rely on. Seek no evil gains: evil
gains are no better than losses.

> Be a friend to him who is your friend,
> and give your company to him that seeks it.
> Give whoso gives, and give not whoso gives not:
> to a giver one gives, to an ungiver none gives.
> Give is good, Snatch bad, a giver of death.

For if a man gives voluntarily, even a big gift, he is glad at
the giving and rejoices in his heart; but if a man takes of
his own accord, trusting in shamelessness, even something little, that puts a frost on the heart.

For if you lay down even a little on a little, and do this
often, even that may well grow big. He who adds to what
is there, wards off burning hunger. What is stored up at

home is not a source of worry; better for things to be
in the house, for what is outside is at risk. It is good to
take from what is available, but sorrow to the heart to
be wanting what is not available. I suggest you reflect
on this.

At the start of a cask or the end of it, take your fill, in
the middle be sparing: parsimony at the bottom is mean.
Let the agreed wage for a man of good will be assured;
and even with your brother, smile but bring in a witness.
Trust and mistrust alike have ruined men. No arse-
rigged woman must deceive your wits with her wily
twitterings when she pokes into your granary; he who
believes a woman, believes cheaters. Hope for an only
son to nourish his father's house, for this is how wealth
waxes in the halls; and to die in old age leaving another
child within.* Yet Zeus can easily provide great prosperity for more: more hands, more work, and greater
surplus.

If your spirit in your breast yearns for riches, do as
follows, and work, work upon work.

> When the Pleiades born of Atlas* rise before the sun,
> begin the reaping; the ploughing, when they set.

For forty nights and days they are hidden, and again as
the year goes round they make their first appearance at
the time of iron-sharpening. This is the rule of the land,
both for those who live near the sea and for those who
live in the winding glens far from the swelling sea, a rich
terrain: naked sow and naked drive the oxen, and naked
reap, if you want to bring in Demeter's works all in due
season, so that you have each crop grow in season.
Otherwise you may find yourself later in want, and beg
at others' houses and achieve nothing—as even now you
have come to me; but I will give you nothing extra or

measure out more. Work, foolish Perses, do the work that the gods have marked out for men, lest one day with children and wife, sick at heart, you look for livelihood around the neighbours and they pay no heed. Twice, three times you may be successful, but if you harass them further, you will achieve nothing, all your speeches will be in vain, and however wide your words range it will be no use.

No, I suggest you reflect on the clearing of your debts and the avoidance of famine. First, a household, a woman, and a ploughing ox—a chattel woman, not wedded, one who could follow the herds. The utilities in the house must all be got ready, lest you ask another, and he refuse, and you be lacking, and the right time go past, and your cultivation suffer. Do not put things off till tomorrow and the next day. A man of ineffectual labour, a postponer, does not fill his granary: it is application that promotes your cultivation, whereas a postponer of labour is constantly wrestling with Blights.

When the keen sun's strength stops scorching and sweltering, after mighty Zeus begins the autumn rain, and human skin feels the change with relief—for then the star Sirius goes but briefly by day above the heads of men who are born to die, having a larger share of the night*—then timber is freest from the worm when hewn by the iron, when it sheds its leaves to the ground and stops putting out shoots. Then do your woodcutting, do not neglect it, a job in season. Cut a mortar to three feet, a pestle to three cubits, an axle to seven feet, that will do very well; or if to eight feet, you may cut a mallet off it too. Cut a three-span wheel for a ten-palm cart.* Many timbers are bent: take a plough-tree home when you find one, searching on the mountain or on the ploughland—one of holm-oak, for that is the firmest for ploughing with oxen when Athene's servant* has fixed it in the stock with dowels and brought it up and fastened it to the pole. Take the trouble to provide yourself with two ploughs at home, a self-treed one and a joined one,* for it is much better so: if you should break one, you can set the other to the oxen. Bay or elm make the most worm-free poles, oak the stock, and holm-oak the plough-tree.

As for the pair of oxen, have nine-year-old males in their prime: their strength will not be feeble. They are the best for working. They are not likely to quarrel in the furrow and break the plough and leave the job there undone. Behind them I would have there go a sturdy man of forty years who has made his meal of a quarter-loaf, an eight-section one; a man who would attend to the work and drive a straight furrow, not still peering about after his fellows but with his mind on the work. And no younger man is better beside him to distribute the seed and avoid oversowing. A younger man is a-flutter after his fellows.

Take heed when you hear the voice of the crane from high in the clouds, making its annual clamour; it brings the signal for ploughing, and indicates the season of winter rains, and it stings the heart of the man with no ox. Then be feeding up the oxen under your roof. For while it is easy to *say* 'Give me a pair of oxen and a cart', it is easy too to refuse: 'But the oxen have work to do'. A man rich in fancy thinks to construct a cart—the fool, he does not know there are a hundred planks to a cart. Attend to laying them up at home beforehand.

As soon as the ploughing-time reveals itself to mortals, then go at it, yourself and your labourers, ploughing dry or wet in ploughing season, getting on with it good and early so that your fields may be full. Go over it first in spring; if it is turned in summer too it will not let you down; and sow the fallow while it is still light soil. Fallow is defence against ruin, the soother of Aïdoneus.* Pray to Zeus of the earth and pure Demeter for Demeter's holy grain to ripen heavy, at the beginning of ploughing when you take the end of the stilt in your hand and come down with a stick on the oxen's back as they pull the yoke-peg by the strapping. And the labourer just behind with the mattock should make it hard work for the birds by covering up the seed. Good order is best for mortal men, and bad order is worst.

In this way the ears may nod towards the earth with thickness, should Olympian Zeus himself grant a successful outcome later, and you may banish the cobwebs from the storage-jars. And I am confident that you will be happy as you draw on the stores under your roof; you will reach the bright spring in prosperity, and not look towards others, rather will another man be in need of you. But if you do not plough the divine earth until the solstice period, you will reap sitting down, gathering little in the crook of your arm, binding opposite ways,* dust-blown, none too cheerful; you will carry it away in a basket, and few will be impressed. Yet the mind of Zeus the aegis-bearer is different at different times, and hard for mortal men to recognize, and if you do plough late, this may be your remedy: when cuckoo first cuckoos in leaves of oak, gladdening mortals on the boundless earth, then hope that Zeus may rain on the third day without intermission, not rising above an ox's hoof nor falling short. So may late-plougher rival early-plougher. But be alert for everything, and do not miss either the coming of bright spring or the seasonal rain.

Pass by the smith's bench and the cosy parlour in winter-time when the cold keeps men from the fields— then an industrious man may do much for his household

—lest in severe weather Helplessness overtakes you together with Poverty, and you squeeze a swollen foot with emaciated hand. Many are the ills that a workshy man, waiting on empty hope, in want of livelihood, complains of to his heart. Hope is no good provider for a needy man sitting in the parlour without substance to depend on. Point out to your labourers while it is still midsummer: 'It will not always be summer. Build your huts.'*

But as for the month of Lenaion*—bad days, ox-flayers all—take precautions against it, and the frosts which are harsh on earth when the North Wind blows. Coming over horse-rearing Thrace, he blows upon the sea and stirs it up, and earth and woodland roar; many are the tall leafy oaks and thick firs in the mountain glens that he bends down to the rich-pastured earth when he falls upon them. The whole immense forest cries aloud, and animals shiver and put their tails under their parts, even those whose skin is covered by fur: even through these he blows cold, shaggy-chested as they are. Through an ox's hide he goes, it does not stop him, and he blows through the hairy goat; but not the flocks, because their hair is unfailing, the North Wind's force does not blow through them. He makes an old man bowl along. And the tender-skinned girl he does not blow through, who stays inside the house with her dear mother, not yet acquainted with the affairs of golden Aphrodite. She washes her fine skin well, rubs it with oil, and lies down in the inner part of the house, all on a winter's day, when the boneless one* crops his foot in his fireless dwelling and his miserable haunts, as the sun does not show him his pasture to make for, but roams toward the community and territory of the black men,* and shines tardier for the Greeks. Then horned and hornless forest-couchers, wretchedly gnashing, run off through the winding glades, and all of those who, when in want of shelter, have thick-set lairs in some rocky cavern, have no other thought on their minds. Then they are like a threelegged man* whose back is broken forward and whose head looks towards the earth: that is how they go as they try to avoid the white snow.

Then put on a covering for your skin according to my instructions, a soft cloak and foot-length tunic: on scant warp wind woof in plenty. Put that about you, so that your whiskers lie still instead of bristling erect over your body. Upon your feet bind shoes of slaughtered oxhide to fit, padding them with fleeces inside; and from the firstling kids, when the cold comes in its season, sew the skins together with ox-gut so that you can put it over your back as protection from rain. Up on your head wear a proper hat so that you do not get your ears wet. For the morning is cold when the North Wind comes down. In the morning, from the starry sky to the earth, a mist extends over the wheat-fields of the fortunate; it draws from the ever-flowing rivers, rises high above the earth on the wind-squall, and sometimes rains towards evening, sometimes blows as the Thracian Northerly scurries the clouds on in dense tumult. Do not wait for that, but finish your work and return home, in case the black cloud from heaven envelops you and wets your skin and soaks your clothes. No, take precautions: this is the worst month, this winter one, bad for livestock and bad for men.

At that time oxen should have half, a man the greater part of his full ration, as the long nights help out. Pay attention to this throughout the year and balance days and nights until Earth, the mother of all, brings forth her varied fruits once more.

When Zeus completes sixty days of winter after the solstice, then the star Arcturus leaves the holy stream of Oceanus and for the first time rises shining just at dusk. After him Pandion's daughter* who laments in the morning twilight, the swallow, comes forth into men's sight as the spring is just established. Do not wait for her before pruning the vines: it is better so.

When the carryhouse* climbs up the plants to escape the Pleiades, then digging of vines is past, it is time to sharpen sickles and wake up the labourers. Avoid shady seats and sleeping till sunrise at harvest time, when the sun parches the skin. At that time get on with it and gather home the harvest, rising before dawn so that your livelihood may be assured.

> For the morning accounts for a third of the work:
> morning forwards the journey, forwards the job,
> morning, whose appearance puts many a man
> on the road, and sets the yoke on many an ox.

When the golden thistle is in flower, and the noisy cicada sitting in the tree pours down its clear song thick and fast from under its wings in the fatiguing summer season, then goats are fattest and wine is best, women are most lustful, but men are weakest, because Sirius parches their head and knees, and their skin is dried out with the heat. Then you want rocky shade and Bibline wine, a milking cake and the goats' last milk,* and meat of a scrub-grazed cow that has not yet calved, and of firstling kids. And after it you want to drink gleaming wine, sitting in the shade, having had the heart's fill of food, facing into a fresh westerly breeze. From a perennial spring that runs away and is unclouded pour three measures of water, and the fourth of wine.*

As for the labourers, spur them to thresh Demeter's

holy grain as soon as mighty Orion appears,* in a well-ventilated place and on a well-rolled floor, and to collect it carefully in the jars with the scoop. When you have stored away all your substance under lock inside the house, I suggest you set about engaging a man with no household, and seek a woman without a child—a working woman with calf at her is a nuisance. And maintain a dog with sharp teeth, not stinting his food, in case a couchbyday* robs you of your property. And bring in hay and rubbish so that your oxen and mules may have enough to last. Then the labourers can rest their poor legs and unyoke the oxen.

When Orion and Sirius come into mid-heaven, Perses, and rose-fingered Dawn meets Arcturus,* then set about cutting off all the grape-clusters for home. Expose them to the sun for ten days and ten nights, cover them over for five, and on the sixth draw merry Dionysus' gift off into jars. But when the Pleiades and Hyades and mighty Orion are setting, then be thinking of ploughing in its season; and may the seed lodge firmly in the earth.

If now the desire to go to sea (disagreeable as it is) has hold of you: when the Pleiades, running before Orion's grim strength, are plunging into the misty sea, then the blasts of every kind of wind rage; at this time do not keep ships on the wine-faced sea, but work the earth assiduously, as I tell you. Pull the ship on to land and pack it with stones all round to withstand the fury of the wet-blowing winds, taking out the plug so that heaven's rains do not cause rot. Lay away all the tackle under lock in your house, tidily stowing the wings* of the seagoing vessel; hang the well-crafted steering-oar up in the smoke; and wait till the time for sailing comes.

Then drag the swift ship to the sea, and in it arrange your cargo fittingly so that you may win profit for your return: just as my father and yours, foolish Perses, used to sail in ships in want of fair livelihood. And one day he came here, making the long crossing from Aeolian Cyme* in his dark ship, not running from riches, nor from wealth and prosperity, but from evil poverty, which Zeus dispenses to men. And he settled near Helicon in a miserable village, Ascra, bad in winter, foul in summer, good at no time.

But you, Perses, must attend to all tasks in season, and in the matter of seafaring above all. Compliment a small ship, but put your cargo in a big one: bigger will be the cargo, bigger the extra gain, provided that the winds withhold their ill blasts.

When you want to escape debt and joyless hunger by turning your blight-witted heart to trade, I will show you the measure of the resounding sea—quite without instruction as I am either in seafaring or in ships; for as to ships, I have never yet sailed the broad sea, except to Euboea from Aulis,* the way the Achaeans once came when they waited through the winter and gathered a great army from holy Greece against Troy of the fair women. There to the funeral games for warlike Amphidamas and to Chalcis I crossed,* and many were the prizes announced and displayed by the sons of that valiant; where I may say that I was victorious in poetry and won a tripod with ring handles. That I dedicated to the Muses of Helicon, in the original place where they set me on the path of fine singing. That is all my experience of dowelled ships, but even so I will tell the design of Zeus the aegis-bearer, since the Muses have taught me to make song without limit.

For fifty days after the solstice, when the summer has entered its last stage, the season of fatigue, then is the time for mortals to sail. You are not likely to smash your ship, nor the sea to destroy the crew, unless it be that of set mind Poseidon the earth-shaker or Zeus king of the immortals wants to destroy them, for in their hands lies the outcome of good and bad things alike. At that time the breezes are well defined and the sea harmless. Then without anxiety, trusting the winds, drag your swift ship into the sea and put all the cargo aboard. But make haste to come home again as quickly as you can, and do not wait for the new wine and the autumn rains, the onset of winter and the fearsome blasts of the South Wind, which stirs up the sea as it comes with heaven's plentiful rains of autumn, and makes the waves rough.

There is another time for men to sail in the spring. As soon as the size of the crow's footprint is matched by the aspect of the leaves on the end of the fig-branch, then the sea is suitable for embarcation. This is the spring sailing. I do not recommend it; it is not to my heart's liking. A snatched sailing: you would have difficulty in avoiding trouble. But men do even that in their folly, because property is as life to wretched mortals. But it is a fearful thing to die among the waves. I suggest you bear all this in mind, as I tell you it.

And do not put all your substance in ships' holds, but leave the greater part and ship the lesser; for it is a fearful thing to meet with disaster among the waves of the sea, and a fearful thing if you put too great a burden up on your cart and smash the axle and the cargo is spoiled. Observe due measure; opportuneness is best in everything.

In due season bring a wife into your house, when you are neither many years short of thirty nor many beyond it: this is your seasonable marriage. As for the woman, she should have four years of ripeness and be married in the fifth.* Marry a virgin, so that you may teach her good ways; and for preference marry her who lives near you, with all circumspection in case your marriage is a joke to the neighbours. For a man acquires nothing better than the good wife, and nothing worse than the bad one, the foodskulk,* who singes a man without a brand, strong though he be, and consigns him to premature old age.

Beware the punishment of the immortal blessed ones.

Do not make a friend on a par with a brother; and if you make one, do not do him ill unprovoked, or offer false tongue-favour. But if he is the one who gives you a disagreeable word or deed, make sure he pays for it double. And if he brings you back into his friendship and is willing to make amends, accept them. It is a worthless man who keeps changing his friends: let *your* disposition not disgrace your appearance.

Do not be known as a man of many guests or of none, as a comrade of the unworthy or a reviler of the worthy. And never venture to insult a man for accursed soul-destroying poverty, which is the dispensation of the blessed ones who are for ever. The tongue's best treasure among men is when it is sparing, and its greatest charm is when it goes in measure. If you speak ill, you may well hear greater yourself. And be not of bad grace at the feast thronged with guests: when all share, the pleasure is greatest and the expense least.

Never pour gleaming wine to Zeus in the morning with unwashed hands, or to the other immortals, for then they pay no heed, and spit out your prayers. Do not urinate standing turned towards the sun; and after sun-set and until sunrise, bear in mind, do not urinate either on the road or off the road walking, nor uncovered: the nights belong to the blessed ones. The godly man of sound sense does it squatting, or going to the wall of the courtyard enclosure. And when your private parts are

stained with semen indoors, do not let them be seen as
you go near the hearth-fire, but avoid it. Do not sow your
stock after returning from a funeral, with its inauspicious
cries, but from a feast shared with the gods. And never
urinate in the waters of rivers that flow to the sea, or at
springs—avoid this strictly—nor void your vapours in
them; that is not advisable. And never step across the
fair-flowing water of ever-running rivers until you have
prayed, looking into the fair stream, after washing your
hands in the lovely clear water. If a man crosses a river
without cleansing his wickedness and his hands, the
gods look askance at him and give him woe later.

Do not from the fivebranched, at the prosperous feast
shared with the gods, cut the sere from the green with
gleaming iron.* And never place the jug above the
mixing-bowl when men are drinking; a dire fate is
attached to that.

When making a house, do not leave it unplaned, in
case you get a raucous crow sitting on it and cawing.* Do
not take from unconsecrated pots to eat or to wash; those
things too carry a penalty. Do not seat upon what may
not be disturbed*, it is not advisable, a child of twelve
days—it makes a man unmanly—nor one of twelve
months, that too is the same. And let not a man cleanse
his skin with woman's washing water, for that too carries
a grim penalty for a time. And do not, when you come
upon a burning sacrifice, balefully find fault with it:* the
god resents that too.

Do as I say; and try to avoid being the object of men's
evil rumour. Rumour is a dangerous thing, light and easy
to pick up, but hard to support and difficult to get rid of.
No rumour ever dies that many folk rumour. She too is
somehow a goddess.

Pay due attention to the days which come from Zeus,*

and indicate them to your labourers—the 30th being the best day of the month to oversee work and distribute rations, when people judge right in celebrating it.* The days ordained by Zeus the resourceful are as follows. Firstly, the 1st and 4th and 7th are holy days (on the 7th Leto gave birth to Apollo of the golden sword), and the 8th and 9th. However, two days of the waxing month are excellent for mortal tasks, the 11th and 12th: both of them good, whether for shearing sheep or for gathering the glad grain, but the 12th is much better than the 11th, as on that day the high-floating spider spins its spans at the full of the day, when the knowing one* gathers its heap. On that day a woman should raise her loom and set up her weaving.

Avoid the 13th of the standing moon for beginning sowing; but it is the best day for bedding in vines. The middle 6th* is very unsuitable for vines, but good for a man's birth; for a girl, however, it is not suitable, either to be born or to marry. Nor again is the first 6th a fit day for a girl to be born, but for gelding kids and rams, and a kindly day for making a sheep-pen; good for a man's birth, but he is likely to have a weakness for impudent abuse, lies, wily pretences, and secret philandering. On the 8th of the month geld a boar or a bellowing bull, and toiling mules on the 12th. On the great 20th, in the full of the day, father a learned man; he will be very close-grown in thought. Also good for a man's birth is the 10th, and for a girl the middle 4th. And on that day tame sheep and shambling curly-horned oxen and the sharp-toothed dog and toiling mules, laying your hand upon them. But make sure to avoid the 4th of the waning and standing month for eating the heart in grief, as it is a very special day. And on the 4th of the month bring a wife into your house, after judging the bird-omens that are best for this undertaking. But avoid the 5ths, for they are difficult and dire: it was on the 5th, they say, that the Erinyes attended Oath at his birth, whom Strife bore as a bane for perjurers.*

On the middle 7th cast Demeter's holy grain on the well-rolled threshing-floor, keeping a sharp eye open; and have a woodcutter cut house planks, and all the ship-timbers that are appropriate for ships. But begin building narrow ships on the 4th.

The middle 9th is a better day towards evening; but the first 9th is altogether harmless for men. It is good for planting and for being born, both for man and woman, and it is never a wholly bad day. Then again, few know that threenines is best of the month for starting on a cask and setting the yoke on the necks of oxen and mules and fleet-footed horses, and for pulling a many-thwarted swift ship into the wine-faced sea; and few call it by its true name. But open a cask on a 4th—a supremely holy day—the middle one.

And few again know that the 21st of the month is best after sunrise; it is worse towards evening.

These are the days that are of great benefit for men on earth. The rest are days of changeable omen, doomless, with nothing to offer. Different people commend different sorts of day, but few know that among those ones 'sometimes a day is a stepmother, sometimes a mother'.

Well with god and fortune is he who works with knowledge of all this, giving the immortals no cause for offence, judging the bird-omens and avoiding trans-gressions.

EXPLANATORY NOTES

1 *Muses of Helicon*: Hesiod locates the goddesses of song on his local mountain in southern Boeotia. Many later poets follow him.

4 *son of Kronos*: Zeus, who is the Muses' father as well as king of the gods.

5–6 *Permessos . . . Olmeios*: streams on Helicon. The Horse's Fountain was said to have been created by a kick of Pegasus' hoof.

11 *the lady Hera of Argos*: Zeus' wife, worshipped especially at Argos. There follows a selection of the most important Olympian gods. Dione is included as the mother of Aphrodite and Leto as mother of Apollo and Artemis.

18 *Iapetos . . . Kronos*: two of the older gods, the Titans, fathers respectively of Prometheus and Zeus.

25 *Olympian Muses*: as related below, they were born on Mount Olympus, where the gods live, and they have their own homes there besides dancing on Helicon.

50 *Giants*: a race of huge and powerful beings, neither men nor gods but closer to the former. They fought against the gods and were defeated.

53 *Pieria*: the region to the north of Olympus, towards Macedonia.

54 *Eleutherae*: a place much nearer Hesiod's home, on Mount Cithaeron between Boeotia and Attica. Memory must have been worshipped there as a goddess of poets.

64 *Graces*: the goddesses who represent all that is delightful—beauty, love, festivity. Their association with the Muses is natural.

77–9 *Clio . . . Calliope*: the names are probably Hesiod's invention, but they remained canonical. They mean roughly: Fame-spreading, Entertaining, Festive, Singing, Dance-delight, Lovely, Rich in Themes, Celestial, Beautiful Voice. It was not until much later that they were individualized as the Muse of History, the Muse of Lyric Poetry, etc.

95 *citharists*: the cithara was a large lyre used by singers to accompany themselves.

116 *the Chasm*: this is the literal meaning of the Greek name Chaos; it does not contain the idea of confusion or disorder.

119 *Tartara*: a plural equivalent of the usual Tartarus, a dark and horrible region far below the earth. See the fuller account at 720–818.

120 *Eros*: the god of sexual love is placed at the beginning of things, being presupposed by all the following generative unions of divine powers.

123 *Erebos*: the realm of darkness, associated with Hades and Tartarus.

133 *Oceanus*: the great river imagined as encircling the earth.

138 *loathed his lusty father*: anticipating the story in 154–82.

139 *Cyclopes*: the name means Circle-eyes. Apart from having only one eye, Hesiod's thunderbolt-manufacturers have little in common with the pastoral Cyclopes described in Book IX of the *Odyssey*.

161 *adamant*: a metal of great hardness used by the gods.

185 *Erinyes*: the goddesses of retribution who exact punishment for murder and other serious crimes. Their birth here is appropriate.

   Giants: see note to line 50.

187 *Meliai*: this means 'ash-trees'. Hesiod perhaps means tree-nymphs in general.

192 *Cythera*: the island near the south-east corner of the Peloponnese. There was a famous shrine of Aphrodite there.

197 *in foam*: the Greek word is *aphros*. Aphrodite's name is associated with it by popular etymology.

200 *genial*: literally 'smile-loving'. Hesiod links *meid*– 'smile' with *mēdea* 'genitals'.

215 *Hesperides*: singing maidens who live in a garden beyond the sunset. One of Heracles' Labours involved getting some of their golden apples.

217 *Furies*: literally Dooms, but in function hard to distinguish from the Erinyes of 185.

223 *Resentment*: the Greek Nemesis does not mean punishment but disapproval or resentment (by gods or men) of disagreeable conduct.

231 *Oath*: the oath that a man swears is conceived as a divine being that will punish him in the event of perjury.

233 *Nereus*: a sea-god, sometimes called the Old Man of the Sea.

237–9 *Thaumas . . . Eurybia*: Thaumas is an obscure figure, the father of Iris and the Harpies. Phorcys is another god identified as the Old Man of the Sea

(*Odyssey* xiii. 96, 345). Ceto's name suggests large sea creatures. Eurybia, Wide Force, will become the wife of the Titan Kreios at 375.

240 *goddess-children*: these are the Nereids, the sea-nymphs. Most of their names are suggested by the sea in one way or another; others express characteristics such as beauty, generosity, foreknowledge.

262 *Nemertes*: 'Truthful'; the same word was applied to Nereus in 235 (there translated 'ne'er-failing' for the sake of the word-play).

266 *Iris*: the gods' messenger, associated with the rainbow.

267 *Harpies*: goddesses of the storm-winds who snatch people away so that they are never seen again.

270 *Old Women*: in Greek *Graiai*. They are so called because of their white hair. In later accounts they have only one eye and one tooth to share among them.

278 *god of the Sable Locks*: Poseidon.

280 *Perseus*: a monster-slayer of Argive myth, like Heracles, who was made a descendant of his. Hesiod evidently knew epic poetry about the exploits of both heroes; he alludes repeatedly to those of Heracles.

282–3 *waters . . . golden sword*: Hesiod derives the names from the Greek words *pēgās* and *chrȳseion aor*.

287 *Geryoneus*: Heracles had to obtain this monstrous person's cattle. The story is referred to again in 979–83.

290 *Erythea*: a mythical island beyond the sunset, later identified with Cadiz.

292 *Tiryns*: the city in the Argolid ruled by Eurystheus, who imposed the Labours on Heracles.

293 *Orthos*: Geryoneus' ferocious dog, whose birth is recorded at 309.

301 *she*: it is not quite clear whether Echidna or Ceto is meant.

304 *Arimi*: mentioned by Homer and Pindar in connection with Typhoeus, Echidna's consort. The ancients were uncertain where to locate the Arimi, but they probably belonged in the east. They are perhaps to be connected with the Aramaeans.

306 *Typhaon*: the same as Typhoeus, the monster described in 821–35.

314 *Lerna*: a place near Argos. The Hydra was a serpent that kept growing more heads as the first were cut off.

315 *in her insatiable wrath . . . Heracles*: she hated him because Zeus had fathered him by another mother (Alcmene). She engineered his subjection to Eurystheus (see note to line 292).

317 *called son of Amphitryon*: Alcmene's husband. He was a cousin of Eurystheus, both being grandsons of Perseus.

318 *advice of Athene driver of armies*: the martial goddess Athene generally helped heroes facing danger, and she stood by Heracles throughout his Labours.

319 *she*: it is not certain whether Echidna or Hydra is meant.

325 *Bellerophon*: another hero who had to overcome a series of dangerous ordeals: see *Iliad* vi. 155–95.

326 *she*: probably Chimaera.

people of Cadmus: the Thebans. The Sphinx sat by the roadside at Thebes and killed every passer-by who could not answer her riddle, 'What creature is two-legged, three-legged, and four-legged at different times?' Finally Oedipus did answer it—'Man'—and that was the end of her.

329 *Nemea*: in the Argolid. The slaying of the lion was generally counted as the first of Heracles' Labours.

331 *Tretos . . . Apesas*: mountains near Nemea.

335 *golden apples*: see note to line 215. Again Hesiod has an exploit of Heracles in mind.

337 *Rivers*: many of those Hesiod lists were known to him from poetry and legend; seven of them belong to the area round Troy and are mentioned in the *Iliad*. The Eridanus was later identified with the Po or the Rhône.

346 *Nymphs*: generally beneficent beings associated with rivers, springs, trees, and mountains. They bring fertility and fortune.

377 *Perses*: this very obscure figure has the same name as Hesiod's brother, who may have been named after him if Hesiod's enthusiasm for Perses' daughter Hecate (411–52) was a family enthusiasm.

384–5 *Aspiration . . . Strength*: personifications of qualities inseparably associated with Zeus as king of the gods.

389 *perennial*: Styx was a stream; see 775–806.

400 *oath of the gods*: they use her water to swear by, as described in 780–806.

406 *Leto*: the mother of Apollo and Artemis, whom she bore in the island of Delos.

409 *Asteria*: an obscure figure. It may be relevant that Asteria is said to have been an old name of Delos.

411 *Hecate*: the section that follows is of especial interest for Hesiod's religious outlook. He sounds like an evangelist for Hecate, who is not mentioned by Homer and seems to have been a relatively new goddess. She has not yet developed the sinister associations that she comes to have in later centuries.

438 *glory on his parents*: the winner would be announced as 'X son of Y', and the whole family would bask in reflected prestige.

440 *till the surly grey*: harvest the sea, that is, go fishing.

441 *Shaker of Earth*: Poseidon, who is god of the sea as well as of earthquakes.

444 *Hermes*: a god especially venerated by herdsmen.

454 *Hestia*: goddess of the hearth.
    Demeter: goddess of cereals.

460 *mother's knees*: women in ancient Greece, as in many societies, gave birth in a kneeling position.

472 *her father's furies*: the avenging spirits of Heaven whom Kronos had castrated and who had threatened retribution in 210.

477 *Lyktos*: a town in Crete near which there was a holy cave associated with the birth of Zeus.

484 *Aegean mountain*: not otherwise recorded.

486 *the Former Gods*: the Titans.

499 *Pytho*: the site of the Delphic oracle.

501 *his father's brothers*: the Cyclopes (139).

514 *Menoitios*: an obscure figure, later said to have fought on the side of the Titans against the younger gods.

536 *Mekone*: said to be an old name of Sicyon in the north-east Peloponnese. Hesiod is presumably relating a myth from that region.

563–4 *would not give to the ash-trees . . . on earth*: in mythology fire is often considered as something stored up in trees.

567 *fennel*: the stalk of the giant fennel contains a dry pith which burns slowly, making it a convenient means of carrying fire from place to place.

571 *Ambidexter*: Hephaestus, the divine smith and general craftsman. In the parallel account of the making of the first woman in *Works and Days* 47–105 she is named Pandora.

617 *their father*: Heaven (147).

632 *Othrys*: the principal mountain on the other side of the Thessalian plain from Olympus.

697 *chthonic Titans*: the adjective anticipates their subsequent location in the underworld.

727 *its neck*: it seems to be imagined in the shape of an enormous storage-jar.

746 *the son of Iapetos*: Atlas.

767 *the chthonic god*: Hades, lord of the dead.

769 *a fearsome hound*: Cerberus (311–12, where he is given fifty heads).

775 *shudder*: alluding to the fact that Styx's name means 'shuddering'.

819 *Cymopolea*: not mentioned elsewhere. Her name Wave-ranger resembles that of some of the Nereids.

860 *Aïdna*: unknown; probably not to be identified with Etna, despite the later story that Typhoeus was

pinned down under the volcano (Pindar, *Pythian Odes* i. 20).

866 *melts in the divine ground*: the smelting of iron ore in the ground is a primitive practice known from India and Africa.

886 *Metis*: one of the Oceanid nymphs (358). Her name means 'resource, cunning', and as a consort of Zeus, now inside him, she represents his possession of that quality.

895 *Tritogeneia*: a name of Athene.

897 *king of gods and men*: by preventing the birth of this potential successor, Zeus ensures that his power is secure for ever.

901 *Themis*: the personification of all that is right and proper in nature and society.

the Watchers: Hesiod has given a new etymologizing meaning and identity to the Horai, who are usually the spirits of seasonal ripeness and growth.

909 *Aglaïa . . . Thalia*: on the Graces see the note to line 64. Their individual names mean Splendour, Good Cheer, and Festivity.

913 *Aïdoneus*: Hades. The story is told at length in the Homeric Hymn to Demeter.

922 *Hebe . . . Eileithyia*: Hebe is the personification of youthful beauty; Ares is the god of war; Eileithyia is the goddess of childbirth.

925 *Atrytone*: a name of Athene.

937 *Cadmus made his wife*: Cadmus was the founder of Thebes. His wedding to the goddess was attended by all the gods. The children of the marriage are listed at 975–8.

938 *Maia*: a nymph who lived on Mount Cyllene in Arcadia.

941 *Dionysus*: god of wine.

948 *Minos' daughter*: Minos was the legendary king of Crete. Ariadne seems originally to have been a Cretan goddess, though in the myth of Theseus and the Minotaur she appears as a mortal princess.

951 *ordeals*: the Labours; see notes at lines 287, 292, 314, 315, 318, 329, 335.

954 *a great feat among the immortals*: probably referring to his assistance in quelling the Giants.

955 *lives free from trouble . . . for all time*: the deification of Heracles is a late myth, ignored in *Iliad* xviii. 117–21 and *Odyssey* xi. 601–27 (but interpolated in the latter passage, ll. 602–4).

957 *Circe*: this goddess appears in the *Odyssey* (x. 135 ff.) living on an island near the sunrise (xii. 3–4).

Aeetes: king of Colchis, the land of the Golden Fleece, in the story of the Argonauts.

969 *Wealth*: conceived in terms of grain stores rather than money. Iasius' sexual union with the corn goddess in a thrice-turned fallow field (i.e. one ready for sowing; see *Works and Days* 462–3) may reflect an ancient agrarian ritual.

976 *Ino, Semele . . . Agaue*: this trio is associated with the Theban birth (940–2) and worship of Dionysus. Agaue plays a leading role in Euripides' *Bacchae* as the bacchant who unwittingly kills her son Pentheus.

977 *Aristaeus*: a son of Apollo. He and Autonoe were the parents of Actaeon.

978 *Polydorus*: ancestor of the later kings of Thebes, including Oedipus.

983 *Erythea*: see note to line 290.

984 *Tithonus*: a Trojan, brother of Priam. Dawn carried him off because he was so lovely, and he remains her consort.

985 *Ethiopians*: a mythical people of the east whom Homer's gods sometimes go away to visit. In one of the lost early epics, the *Aethiopis*, Memnon brought an Ethiopian force to assist the Trojans, but was slain by Achilles.

Emathion: an obscure figure.

986 *Cephalus*: a son of Hermes. Dawn carried him off too.

987 *Phaëthon*: apparently a different person from the Phaëthon who was son of the Sun and who drove the Sun's chariot one day with disastrous results.

993 *the son of Aeson*: Jason.

the daughter: Medea.

996 *Pelias*: king of Iolcus in Thessaly. Fearing Jason because of an oracle, he sent him to obtain the Golden Fleece, a quest which involved many dangers.

1001 *Medeios*: mythical ancestor of the Medes.

1002 *Philyra*: a nymph with whom Kronos had intercourse in the form of a horse. Her child Chiron was accordingly a centaur, half horse and half man. He was learned and benign, and several heroes are said to have been educated by him.

1004 *Phocus*: ancestor of the Phocians of central Greece.

1005 *Aeacus*: son of Zeus and the nymph Aegina, and

first king of the island of Aegina. Peleus was another son of his by a different wife.

1009   *Anchises*: a second cousin of Priam. The story of Aphrodite's visit to him is told in the Homeric Hymn to Aphrodite. where she foretells the birth of Aeneas and his inheritance of the Trojan throne after the fall of Priam.

1011–12   *Circe . . . Odysseus*: he shares her bed for a year in the *Odyssey* (x. 347, 467), but the idea that she bore him children is new and fanciful.

1015   *Holy Isles*: the poet has a vague notion of islands away to the north-west of Greece, and of Tyrrhenians (Etruscans) and Latins located in that direction. Latinus' domination over Etruscans inverts historical reality. The significance of Agrius (Savage) is uncertain.

1017   *Calypso*: again building on the *Odyssey*, in which Odysseus passes seven years with Calypso on her island Ogygia.

11 *not only one Strife-brood*: Hesiod modifies what he had said in *Theogony* 225. He now realizes that there is a good kind of Strife as well as the bad kind.

41 *mallow and asphodel*: the cheapest and plainest of comestibles. Even such poor fare is better than a loaded table that depends on dishonesty.

45 *up in the smoke*: to preserve it when not in use. The point is that one would not need to engage in sea-trading to support oneself.

48 *tricked him*: as related in *Theogony* 535–57.

66 *painful yearning and consuming obsession*: these feelings that woman arouses in others are treated as constituents of herself.

68 *dog-killer*: Hermes was the patron of thieves, who sometimes find it expedient to eliminate watch-dogs.

97 *remained there*: Hesiod has not given his jar a consistent symbolic meaning. He means that hope remains among men as the one antidote to suffering.

142 *they too have honour*: the Silver men are identified with the unknown occupants of certain ancient tombs that are regarded with superstitious reverence.

146 *no eaters of corn*: agriculture is a normal feature of civilized life. The Bronze men, it is implied, lived on what grew wild, supplemented by meat.

151 *iron was not available*: the myth incorporates a popular memory of the archaeological Bronze Age. Iron-working came to Greece in the eleventh century BC.

In epic poetry bronze remained the normal material for spear- and arrow-heads, although in life they had come to be made of iron.

160 *demigods*: because they were descended from unions between gods and mortal women. These were the individually named heroes of epic legend.

163 *Oedipus' flocks*: the first great attack on Thebes resulted from the quarrel between Oedipus' sons Polynices and Eteocles over his throne and estates. The attack failed, with the two brothers killing each other, but in a revival of the conflict in the next generation the city fell. The wars at Thebes and Troy were the dominant subjects of epic tradition.

173 *thrice a year*: at this point two papyri preserve fragments of an ancient interpolation according to which Kronos, released from Tartarus by Zeus, rules over these Heroes in their distant paradise. Compare Pindar, *Olympian Odes*, ii. 70.

216 *Blights*: afflictions or calamities, here imagined as dangers on the road.

219 *Oath . . . crooked judgments*: see note to *Theogony* 231.

233 *acorns . . . bees at its centre*: perhaps a rationalization of the mythical idea of paradise trees that bear abundant fruit and run with honey.

299 *of Zeus' stock*: the family must have claimed descent from one of the ancient heroes.

345 *neighbours . . . gird themselves*: in an emergency those near at hand can come just as they are, without a moment's delay.

378 *another child within*: a grandson, to give hope of continuity for the future.

383 *born of Atlas*: the seven Pleiades were identified with seven nymphs, daughters of Atlas.

419 *larger share of the night*: the intense heat of the 'Dog days' in July and August was supposed to be due to Sirius' being in the sky all day with the sun.

426 *a three-span wheel for a ten-palm cart*: the measurements are approximately 69 cm and 76 cm. The first is probably the diameter of the wheel, the second perhaps the length of the cart.

430 *Athene's servant*: a joiner.

433 *a self-treed one and a joined one*: one having the tree and stock all in one piece (from a lucky find), another made from two pieces.

464 *soother of Aïdoneus*: Hades is inimical to growth; he tries to keep Persephone with him in the underworld. Leaving a field fallow for a year helps to overcome his resistance.

481 *opposite ways*: with ears at both ends of the sheaf to keep the band from slipping off, the straw being so short.

503 *your huts*: temporary winter shelters for the labourers.

504 *Lenaion*: January–February.

524 *the boneless one*: the octopus.

527 *the black men*: in Africa.

533 *threelegged man*: as in the Sphinx's riddle, an old man who uses a stick.

568 *Pandion's daughter*: Philomela, who was turned into a swallow at the conclusion of the tragic tale related by Ovid, *Metamorphoses*, vi. 424–674, among others.

571 *carryhouse*: the snail.

590 *last milk*: the goats bore their kids in the spring and ceased lactation a few months later. The late milk was considered the best.

596 *three measures . . of wine*: the Greeks drank their wine heavily diluted.

598 *as soon as mighty Orion appears*: that is, rises just before dawn (in the second half of June).

605 *couchbyday*: a burglar who works at night.

610 *Dawn meets Arcturus*: when Arcturus rises just before dawn (early September).

628 *wings*: classical poets use this metaphor of both sails and oars.

636 *Cyme*: on the coast of Asia Minor, just south of Lesbos.

651 *Aulis*: on the eastern shore of Boeotia at the closest point to Euboea, the channel being only some 65 metres wide. Aulis was celebrated as the place where the Greek fleet assembled before sailing against Troy.

655 *to Chalcis I crossed*: a town of major importance just across the strait from Aulis. Amphidamas is said to have been a hero of the war fought by Chalcis against her neighbour Eretria for possession of the plain of Lelanton.

698 *four years . . . the fifth*: after beginning menstruation.

704 *focdskulk*: she hovers about looking for opportunities to get her hands on more food than her husband allows her.

742–3 *from the fivebranched . . . iron*: that is, cut your nails.

747 *a raucous crow . . . cawing*: a bad omen, probably presaging a death.

750 *what may not be disturbed*: tombs.

756 *find fault with it*: criticize the sacrificers for meanness.

765 *come from Zeus*: as ruler of the world, Zeus is responsible for the different characteristics attaching to different days of the month.

768 *judge right in celebrating it*: months oscillated between 29 and 30 days as communities tried to keep their calendars in step with the moon, but the last day was called the 30th in either case. There would often be uncertainty about whether to have the '30th' one day or two days after the 28th.

778 *the knowing one*: the ant.

782 *middle 6th*: Hesiod calls the days from 14th to 19th 'the middle 4th' and so on. Those in the last third of the month, unless they have special names, are called '4th (etc.) of the waning month'; but they were probably counted backwards from the 30th, this '4th', for example, being the 27th, not the 24th.

804 *bane for perjurers*: see the note to *Theogony* 231. The Erinyes, the goddesses of vengeance, assist at Oath's birth because they too have a connection with the punishment of perjury.

THE WORLD'S CLASSICS

A Select List

SERGEI AKSAKOV: A Russian Gentleman
Translated by J. D. Duff
Edited by Edward Crankshaw

A Russian Schoolboy
Translated by J. D. Duff
Introduction by John Bayley

HANS ANDERSEN: Fairy Tales
Translated by L. W. Kingsland
Introduction by Naomi Lewis
Illustrated by Vilhelm Pedersen and Lorenz Frølich

ARTHUR J. ARBERRY (Transl.): The Koran

LUDOVICO ARIOSTO: Orlando Furioso
Translated by Guido Waldman

ARISTOTLE: The Nicomachean Ethics
Translated by David Ross

JANE AUSTEN: Emma
Edited by James Kinsley and David Lodge

Mansfield Park
Edited by James Kinsley and John Lucas

Northanger Abbey, Lady Susan, The Watsons,
and Sanditon
Edited by John Davie

ROBERT BAGE: Hermsprong
Edited by Peter Faulkner

WILLIAM BECKFORD: Vathek
Edited by Roger Lonsdale

R. D. BLACKMORE: Lorna Doone
Edited by Sally Shuttleworth

KEITH BOSLEY (Transl.): The Kalevala

JAMES BOSWELL: Life of Johnson
The Hill/Powell edition, revised by David Fleeman
Introduction by Pat Rogers

MARY ELIZABETH BRADDON: Lady Audley's Secret
Edited by David Skilton

CHARLOTTE BRONTË: Jane Eyre
Edited by Margaret Smith

Shirley
Edited by Margaret Smith and Herbert Rosengarten

EMILY BRONTË: Wuthering Heights
Edited by Ian Jack

GEORG BÜCHNER:
Danton's Death, Leonce and Lena, Woyzeck
Translated by Victor Price

JOHN BUNYAN: The Pilgrim's Progress
Edited by N. H. Keeble

FANNY BURNEY: Camilla
Edited by Edward A. Bloom and Lilian D. Bloom

THOMAS CARLYLE: The French Revolution
Edited by K. J. Fielding and David Sorensen

LEWIS CARROLL: Alice's Adventures in Wonderland
and Through the Looking Glass
Edited by Roger Lancelyn Green
Illustrated by John Tenniel

GEOFFREY CHAUCER: The Canterbury Tales
Translated by David Wright

ANTON CHEKHOV: The Russian Master and Other Stories
Translated by Ronald Hingley

Ward Number Six and Other Stories
Translated by Ronald Hingley

J. SHERIDAN LE FANU: Uncle Silas
Edited by W. J. McCormack

CHARLOTTE LENNOX: The Female Quixote
Edited by Margaret Dalziel
Introduction by Margaret Anne Doody

LEONARDO DA VINCI: Notebooks
Edited by Irma A. Richter

MIKHAIL LERMONTOV: A Hero of our Time
Translated by Vladimar Nabokov with Dmitri Nabokov

MATTHEW LEWIS: The Monk
Edited by Howard Anderson

NICCOLÒ MACHIAVELLI: The Prince
Edited by Peter Bondanella and Mark Musa
Introduction by Peter Bondanella

HENRY MACKENZIE: The Man of Feeling
Edited by Brian Vickers

KATHERINE MANSFIELD: Selected Stories
Edited by D. M. Davin

CHARLES MATURIN: Melmoth the Wanderer
Edited by Douglas Grant
Introduction by Chris Baldick

HERMAN MELVILLE: The Confidence-Man
Edited by Tony Tanner

Moby Dick
Edited by Tony Tanner

GEORGE MEREDITH: Beauchamp's Career
Edited by Margaret Harris

The Ordeal of Richard Feverel
Edited by John Halperin

PROSPER MÉRIMÉE: Carmen and Other Stories
Translated by Nicholas Jotcham

MICHELANGELO: Life, Letters, and Poetry
Translated by George Bull with Peter Porter

MOLIÈRE: Don Juan and Other Plays
Translated by George Graveley and Ian Maclean

GEORGE MOORE: Esther Waters
Edited by David Skilton

JOHN HENRY NEWMAN: Loss and Gain
Edited by Alan G. Hill

MARGARET OLIPHANT:
The Doctor's Family and Other Stories
Edited by Merryn Williams

OVID: Metamorphoses
Translated by A. D. Melville
Introduction and Notes by E. J. Kenney

WALTER PATER: Marius the Epicurean
Edited by Ian Small

THOMAS LOVE PEACOCK: Headlong Hall and Gryll Grange
Edited by Michael Baron and Michael Slater

FRANCESCO PETRARCH:
Selections from the Canzoniere and Other Works
Translated by Mark Musa

EDGAR ALLAN POE: Selected Tales
Edited by Julian Symons

JEAN RACINE: Britannicus, Phaedra, Athaliah
Translated by C. H. Sisson

ANN RADCLIFFE: The Italian
Edited by Frederick Garber

The Mysteries of Udolpho
Edited by Bonamy Dobrée

The Romance of the Forest
Edited by Chloe Chard

SAMUEL RICHARDSON: Sir Charles Grandison
Edited by Jocelyn Baines

M. E. SALTYKOV-SHCHEDRIN: The Golovlevs
Translated by I. P. Foote

PAUL SALZMAN (Ed.):
An Anthology of Elizabethan Prose Fiction

SIR WALTER SCOTT: The Heart of Midlothian
Edited by Claire Lamont

Waverley
Edited by Claire Lamont

MARY SHELLEY: Frankenstein
Edited by M. K. Joseph

PERCY BYSSHE SHELLEY: Zastrozzi *and* St. Irvyne
Edited by Stephen Behrendt

SIR PHILIP SIDNEY:
The Countess of Pembroke's Arcadia (The Old Arcadia)
Edited by Katherine Duncan-Jones

CHARLOTTE SMITH: The Old Manor House
Edited by Anne Henry Ehrenpreis

TOBIAS SMOLLETT: The Expedition of Humphry Clinker
Edited by Lewis M. Knapp
Revised by Paul-Gabriel Boucé

Peregrine Pickle
Edited by James L. Clifford
Revised by Paul-Gabriel Boucé

LAURENCE STERNE: A Sentimental Journey
Edited by Ian Jack

Tristram Shandy
Edited by Ian Campbell Ross

ROBERT LOUIS STEVENSON: Kidnapped and Catriona
Edited by Emma Letley

The Strange Case of Dr. Jekyll and Mr. Hyde
and Weir of Hermiston
Edited by Emma Letley

BRAM STOKER: Dracula
Edited by A. N. Wilson

R. S. SURTEES: Mr. Facey Romford's Hounds
Edited by Jeremy Lewis

Mr. Sponge's Sporting Tour
Introduction by Joyce Cary

JONATHAN SWIFT: Gulliver's Travels
Edited by Paul Turner

A Tale of a Tub and Other Works
Edited by Angus Ross and David Woolley

WILLIAM MAKEPEACE THACKERAY: Barry Lyndon
Edited by Andrew Sanders

Vanity Fair
Edited by John Sutherland

LEO TOLSTOY: Anna Karenina
Translated by Louise and Aylmer Maude
Introduction by John Bayley

War and Peace (in two volumes)
Translated by Louise and Aylmer Maude
Edited by Henry Gifford

ANTHONY TROLLOPE: The American Senator
Edited by John Halperin

The Belton Estate
Edited by John Halperin

Cousin Henry
Edited by Julian Thompson

The Eustace Diamonds
Edited by W. J. McCormack

The Kellys and the O'Kellys
Edited by W. J. McCormack
Introduction by William Trevor

Orley Farm
Edited by David Skilton

Rachel Ray
Edited by P. D. Edwards

The Warden
Edited by David Skilton

IVAN TURGENEV: First Love and Other Stories
Translated by Richard Freeborn

VILLIERS DE L'ISLE-ADAM: Cruel Tales
Translated by Robert Baldick
Edited by A. W. Raitt

VIRGIL: The Aeneid
Translated by C. Day Lewis
Edited by Jasper Griffin

The Eclogues and The Georgics
Translated by C. Day Lewis
Edited by R. O. A. M. Lyne

HORACE WALPOLE: The Castle of Otranto
Edited by W. S. Lewis

IZAAK WALTON and CHARLES COTTON:
The Compleat Angler
Edited by John Buxton
Introduction by John Buchan

MRS HUMPHREY WARD: Robert Elsmere
Edited by Rosemary Ashton

OSCAR WILDE: Complete Shorter Fiction
Edited by Isobel Murray

The Picture of Dorian Gray
Edited by Isobel Murray

MARY WOLLSTONECRAFT:
Mary *and* The Wrongs of Woman
Edited by Gary Kelly

ÉMILE ZOLA:
The Attack on the Mill and other stories
Translated by Douglas Parmeé

A complete list of Oxford Paperbacks, including The World's
Classics, OPUS, Past Masters, Oxford Authors, Oxford
Shakespeare, and Oxford Paperback Reference, is available in the
UK from the Arts and Reference Publicity Department (RS),
Oxford University Press, Walton Street, Oxford OX2 6DP.

In the USA, complete lists are available from the Paperbacks
Marketing Manager, Oxford University Press, 200 Madison
Avenue, New York, NY 10016.

Oxford Paperbacks are available from all good bookshops. In case
of difficulty, customers in the UK can order direct from Oxford
University Press Bookshop, Freepost, 116 High Street, Oxford,
OX1 4BR, enclosing full payment. Please add 10 per cent of
published price for postage and packing.